Prai
Tracing

"Phyllis Kester has written a fascinating account of her family's tragedies and triumphs. It rings with authenticity. All the while, Phyllis has been aware of God's love and faithfulness. This book is hard to put down."

—Lowell Beach Sykes, Pastor Emeritus
Rivermont Evangelical Presbyterian Church

"Troubles either make us bitter or better. God taught Phyllis Kester that the way to *better* comes through recognizing and remembering His provisions in the midst of tragedy. This book will be of great benefit to you as you face your crises."

—Jerry Kroll, Pastor Emeritus
Heritage Baptist Church

"Phyllis Kester has lived this story! Her book illustrates how a genuine tragedy spurred her family to living lives of deeper faith. The Bible teaches us that "without faith, it is impossible to please God." Marvel at the minute details of how God sent people seemingly out of nowhere to rescue, care, and transport this family in their hour of crisis back to normal living with a fresh revelation of their loving God."

—*Jack Hill,*
World Outreach Ministries

"There is no human explanation for all that happened. . . . I know of no one who has a deeper awareness and understanding of the grace of God, his sovereign and providential care than Phyllis." (*from the foreword*)
—*Harvey D Hartman, ThD, Retired professor*
of Biblical Studies Liberty University

Tracing God's Hand

Tracing God's Hand

Finding Hope and
Freedom from Fear

Phyllis Smith Kester

ILLUMIFY
MEDIA.COM

Tracing God's Hand

Copyright © 2023 by Phyllis Smith Kester

All rights reserved. No part of this book may be reproduced in any form or by any means—whether electronic, digital, mechanical, or otherwise—without permission in writing from the publisher, except by a reviewer, who may quote brief passages in a review.

All Scripture quotations, unless otherwise indicated, are taken from The Holy Bible, English Standard Version®, Copyright © 2016 by Crossway Bibles, a division of Good News Publishers. Used by permission. All rights reserved.

Scripture quotations noted as NJB are taken from The New Jerusalem Bible, published and copyright 1985 by Darton, Longman & Todd Ltd and *Les Editions du Cerf*, and used by permission of the publishers.

Scripture quotations noted as NJKV are taken from the New King James Version. Copyright © 1979, 1980, 1982 by Thomas Nelson, Inc. Used by permission. All rights reserved.

The views and opinions expressed in this book are those of the author and do not necessarily reflect the official policy or position of Illumify Media Global.

Published by
Illumify Media Global
www.IllumifyMedia.com
"Let's bring your book to life!"

Paperback ISBN: 978-1-959099-08-6
Typeset by Art Innovations (http://artinnovations.in/)
Cover design by Debbie Lewis

Printed in the United States of America

This book is dedicated to

MONTY CHARLES KESTER

I thank God for placing Monty in my life as my soulmate for fifty-seven years—a man who gave unfailing love, support, and sacrifice for his loved ones. He initiated many adventures I would never have started on my own, passionately prayed for me, listened with patience, and asked insightful questions while encouraging and challenging me to stretch to be all that God would have me be.

CONTENTS

FOREWORD

HARVEY D. HARTMAN, TH.D.

I met Phyllis Kester and her husband, Monty, in 1988 when they joined the mathematics faculty at Liberty University, where I was a professor of biblical studies in the School of Religion. Because of classroom shortages at the time, most faculty were assigned to teach their courses wherever classrooms were available. Various times Phyllis was assigned to teach in one of the classrooms very near my office in the School of Religion building. I do not recall her ever complaining about the trek across campus from her office to the classroom. I do remember her smiling and saying, "Have chalk, will travel."

Over most of the many years since we met, we have attended Sunday School together. When I began teaching the Legacy Builders discipleship class at Heritage Baptist Church, Phyllis and Monty became faithful members.

When given the opportunity to reflect upon the past, in retrospect we are often able to evaluate decisions and events so much better than at the time when they occurred. We often refer to it as hindsight, and if our renewed perception is exceptionally clear, we call it 20-20 hindsight. We can experience this hindsight with a review of a variety of circumstances— of business, academic, and parenting decisions, and also with theological perspectives. Just ask Joseph, the favored son of Jacob, who was hated by his brothers and was sold as a slave into Egypt. Many years later, his needy brothers faced him in Egypt. He now occupied a powerful position in Egypt, but instead of taking revenge on them for their evil actions against him many years earlier, Joseph reviewed and evaluated all that had happened to him in the intervening years. Though he would not have desired or chosen all the hardship and trials he had experienced, he now clearly saw the hand of God in them. He was able to say, "God sent me here" (Gen. 45:5, 7), and some years later he reaffirmed to his brothers that "God intended it for good" (Gen. 50:20).

Phyllis Kester, in a different, yet somewhat similar manner, has reviewed for us some very difficult times in her life. Never would she have asked God to involve her family in an automobile accident that almost took her husband's life, but as she reflected on how God miraculously spared his life and then time and again providentially guided them to the right medical facilities and provided them with help from total strangers, there is no human explanation for all that happened. Phyllis will concur with Joseph, "It was God."

Phyllis asked me to read her first draft as she wrote *Tracing God's Hand*. For years I had heard her speak of "the wreck," an automobile accident involving her and her husband and boys, but not until after having read her manuscript did I understand the severity of her husband's injuries and how that event continued to shape Phyllis and Monty into the exemplary Christians that I knew them to be. I know of no one who has a deeper awareness and understanding of the grace of God, his sovereign and providential care, than Phyllis.

As I reflect on her story, I am reminded of the testimony of the biblical prophet Jeremiah. Bad things had happened to him and his people, especially in Jerusalem. Yet he was able to say,

But this I call to mind,
and therefore I have hope:

The steadfast love of the Lord never ceases;
his mercies never come to an end;
they are new every morning;
great is your faithfulness.
"The Lord is my portion," says my soul,
"therefore, I will hope in him."
(Lamentations 3:21–24)

Like the prophet Jeremiah, Phyllis had her own set of bad things happen to her, but like the prophet, she did not lose sight of God's steadfast love, mercies, and faithfulness. And she never lost faith in Him.

I am a lover of the old hymns of the faith. I was delighted to see that Phyllis chose a meaningful and appropriate hymn to conclude the chapters of her book. But there is another hymn that kept coming to mind as I read through these pages, because it supports Phyllis's story from beginning to end. It is a hymn written and published by Fanny Crosby in 1875.

All the way my Savior leads me;
What have I to ask beside?
Can I doubt His tender mercy,
Who through life has been my guide?
Heav'nly peace, divinest comfort,
Here by faith in Him to dwell!
For I know, whate'er befall me,
Jesus doeth all things well;
For I know, whate'er befall me,
Jesus doeth all things well.

All the way my Savior leads me,
Cheers each winding path I tread;
Gives me grace for every trial,
Feeds me with the living bread.
Though my weary steps may falter,
And my soul athirst may be,
Gushing from the rock before me,
Lo! A spring of joy I see;
Gushing from the rock before me,
Lo! A spring of joy I see.

All the way my Savior leads me
O the fullness of His love!
Perfect rest to me is promised

In my Father's house above.
When my spirit, clothed immortal,
Wings its flight to realms of day
This my song through endless ages—
Jesus led me all the way;
This my song through endless ages—
*Jesus led me all the way.**

---

* "All the Way My Savior Leads Me," words by Fanny Crosby, public domain, 1875, http://www.hymntime.com/tch/htm/a/l/t/h/altheway.htm.

In 2018 my husband and I were eating lunch with some friends when the conversation strayed onto the topic of car wrecks. I told about some unusual incidents related to our 1975 car wreck and described a few of the startling solutions that solved certain problems.

After we finished eating and rose to leave, one of our companions, Dr. Driscoll, emphatically stated—almost like a command—"Phyllis, you've got to write all that down so I can share it with other people for their encouragement."

I smiled and thought, *Sure. Maybe. Someday.*

When Covid hit with all its lockdowns, the Lord brought that incident back to my mind. Suddenly I had lots of time inside my apartment, and I thought, *Why not? I certainly have the time now. Besides, it would fill in all the gaps for friends and family who only know bits and pieces of our story.*

Maybe—as I was challenged to do—it will encourage you now and as you go through difficult days.

CHAPTER 1

Jaws of Life

Jesus said,
Peace I leave with you; my peace I give to you.
Not as the world gives do I give to you.
Let not your hearts be troubled,
neither let them be afraid.
–JOHN 14:27

Our blue Mercury Marquis station wagon snaked north on US 259 in southeastern Oklahoma with my husband at the wheel. We had folded down the back seat of our station wagon to serve as a bed so our six- and seven-year-old sons could sleep as we drove. On this Wednesday night before Thanksgiving 1975, we intended to drive from Houston, Texas, to

1

Siloam Springs, Arkansas, a 550-mile trip by car. It was now six o'clock, and we'd been in the car for hours since watching our sons play their parts in the school's Thanksgiving program. Both boys had finished eating and were stretched out with their heads on their pillows.

We had crossed the Texas-Oklahoma state line and stopped for gas at Idabel, Oklahoma. Having driven this winding, two-lane road before, we knew we would reach our destination in Northwest Arkansas at about 10 p.m.

We finished eating supper in the car, and I put away the food. Bending down to put an empty milk carton into the trash sack at my feet, I suddenly felt tension in the air.

Monty abruptly shifted on the front bench seat.

Alarmed, I lifted my head to peep over the dashboard and froze.

There's a headlight right in front of me! What's—

The violence of an explosive crash of metal vehicles engulfed me.

All went black.

Somewhere down a long dark tunnel of unconsciousness, I heard terrified screams. "Mommy! Mommy! Daddy's dead!"

With the boys' terrified screams ringing in my head, my maternal instinct rose to override my personal circumstances. I fought to get to my frightened children. However, the sudden combined 150-mile-per-hour, head-on impact tossed luggage, toys, and Christmas presents to the front on top of me. Crumpled under a heap of stuff and disoriented, I didn't know up from down.

Must get to the boys!

Clawing and thrashing in the darkness—it felt like an eternity. I couldn't find a way out of my dark-tunnel nightmare. Apparently my wild flailing hit the door handle for suddenly the door swung open, and I abruptly landed like a sack of potatoes on the cold ground.

Shivering as the frigid air engulfed me, I was grateful the sudden bitter cold cleared my head. Monty was motionless. His head had rolled backward on the back of his seat.

He looks dead. There's no time to waste.

The back car door wouldn't open, but with my help David found a gap he could wiggle through to my open front door. As I began carefully extricating both children from the vehicle, they bombarded me with questions about their father. I gathered them in my arms and said, "Daddy's in the Lord's hands. All we can do is pray for him." So we did.

I grabbed a handy box lid from the car and handed it to the boys. "Your Legos are scattered all over. Get busy picking them up and put them in this lid. You'll want them later."

With them occupied, I went up onto the road to flag a motorist. In 1975 cell phones were not widely available, and smart phones didn't exist. The Citizens' Band (CB) radio was how people communicated, especially between emergency vehicles.

As a result of the frequent fatalities on this particular section of road, the Oklahoma Highway Department was in the process of straightening this stretch of US 259, commonly known as "Dead-Man's Curve." Because buildings had been built inside the sharp, almost 90 degree, curve, approaching traffic was hidden from both directions. We had approached the blind curve on the two-lane road from the south, while the pickup truck that hit us had come from the west on the new four-lane straightaway.

When the pickup suddenly appeared in our lane, Monty instinctively steered to the right to get out of the way—but the approaching vehicle was leaving the highway with us. We didn't realize the driver had lost control because of his excessive speed.

The police later told us the other driver had put a new motor in an old pickup truck and was test driving it to see how fast it would go. They further said they could easily guarantee the truck was going at a minimum of 85 miles per hour and most likely much more. They were amazed we survived. Fortunately, we were in a heavy Mercury Marquis Station Wagon, but in the 1970s airbags had not yet become standard equipment in cars.

People and vehicles began arriving on the scene almost immediately. Since we were out in the country south of Broken Bow, Oklahoma, there were no street lights. As the locals arrived, they systematically arranged their cars and trucks so headlights were shining on us.

They must have done this before. They seem so practiced—almost organized.

Monty groaned.

He's still alive!

I scrambled back into the front seat to reach through the jagged metal to hold his head still and to protect him. He seemed to want to thrash around, but his head was the only thing he could move for he was wrapped in a metal cocoon. I slipped my hands through gaps in the metal to hold his head still while I talked to him.

"Hold still, Honey. Help is on the way. The rest of us are safe. And we're going to get you to a hospital."

I can't believe there's just enough space for me to move my hands all around his head. It's almost as if he had on a protective helmet.

He never said a word, only moaned from time to time. I stayed in the car to hold his head motionless and tried to comfort him. I didn't want him to bang against any of the pointed pieces of metal surrounding him.

I became aware that our car's hood had crashed through the front windshield, but the corner of the hood had folded over.

Hmmm, it's the same way that I fold the corner of a page to mark my place in a book.

The fold of the hood was a fraction of an inch from Monty's forehead. My pulse quickened. *If it hadn't been folded, it would have decapitated him!*

By now the police and others were swarming around us. An elderly couple entertained and distracted Charles and David. They asked permission to take the boys to their car to keep them warm, and I agreed. Others were milling around mumbling about how they had never seen a wreck like this. We were hit from the front, yet we had not burned. A few observers were cautioning others because they could see and smell gasoline.

A relatively new piece of equipment at the time called the Jaws of Life arrived on the scene, and several men rushed forward to find a way to extract Monty from the crumpled metal. I was told these men had recently completed their training and were the only rescue team in all of Oklahoma at that time. They *just happened* to be nearby and heard someone on a CB mention our accident. Using their Jaws of Life, they began prying, bending, and cutting pieces of the car to open Monty's cocoon enough to free him. It looked and sounded frightening. I was totally unfamiliar with the Jaws of Life and how they operated. Others were telling me that what they were doing was a good thing.

O Lord, if he's not paralyzed from this wreck, please don't let them cause him any harm with what they're doing.

A feeling of peace enveloped me like a warm blanket. Regardless of what the circumstances

looked like, at a deeper level I understood God was
in control of our situation. It was almost as if I had
practiced this whole scenario and was just playing a
role I already knew. But what had prepared me for
this?

> *When peace, like a river, attendeth my way,*
> *When sorrows like sea billows roll;*
> *Whatever my lot, Thou has taught me to say,*
> *"It is well, it is well, with my soul."** *

---

* "It Is Well with My Soul," words by Horatio G. Spafford, public domain, 1876, http://www.hymntime.com.

CHAPTER 2

Flashback

Do not be conformed to this world,
but be transformed by the renewal of your mind,
that by testing you may discern
what is the will of God,
what is good and acceptable and perfect.
—ROMANS 12:2

Part 1: Forged by Fire

Nothing happens in isolation. Today, we are each the accumulation of many decisions and their consequences—hence by the time of the wreck, Monty and I showed the results of many previous choices.

He and I met during graduate school at Oklahoma State University. We were both graduate teaching assistants in mathematics, and he was one of my assigned office mates. Soon we became coffee buddies, then we progressed to kindred spirits and to marriage in 1964.

Phyllis and her Grandmother Hays

Years earlier, during my preschool years, my maternal grandmother Hays had lived with my family. Daily, I was privileged to watch her, listen to her specific prayers, and see them answered with my own eyes. Never before, or since, have I met anyone who trusted God so completely. This loving, humble widow reared five boys and two girls in rural Oklahoma before and during the Great Depression. She was a living illustration of a woman who knew God as her loving, heavenly Father and friend. Her walk with God whetted my appetite to know the same prayer-answering-living-God of the Bible she knew, and it set me on a lifelong journey of seeking my own experience with God. Over the years, the Lord drew me to Himself, opened my eyes, and I too became a Christian. I had no idea of all the ramifications that would flow from that decision because the slow growth process took place over my lifetime.

In my early twenties I found that spending time in prayer and reading Scripture was easy when single and living on my own. But as Monty and I dated and were married, I found it more challenging to spend the same amount of personal time with the Lord. A slow process of small, innocent choices— long conversations, spending more and more time together—led me into spiritual drifting. I wished to spend more time with the seen (Monty) rather than the unseen (my Creator).

After a short teaching period in Texas and Arkansas, we returned to Oklahoma State University in 1972 for Monty to complete his interrupted doctoral program. Yet now we had two blond-headed boys in diapers.

Moving to OSU marked the beginning of two-and-a-half years of all types of crises, with at least one major one each month. This brought about a change in my careless attitude concerning my time with God. First, our two-year-old Charles' ballooning hydrocele and enlarging scrotum turned our world topsy turvy for over a year before eventually requiring surgery.

Then David our younger one—always the active explorer—came screaming toward the house from our supposedly safe, fenced backyard. He was crying and pointing to four large puncture holes in his small forearm. A little past one year of age and not talking much, he couldn't tell me what happened. We had multiple doctors and veterinarians look at the four strange holes as we tried to determine what had happened to him. We were informed that local authorities had found rabid skunks and raccoons in town during the previous several months. Since rabies is lethal if ignored, we concluded that our toddler should take the multiple-week series of painful rabies shots as a precaution, even though no one knew what had bitten him.

We were not alone. Each day as I pulled into the parking lot of the pediatrician administering the rabies shots, I would hear other children screaming and crying because they knew the painful injection was about to happen. This pattern was repeated with the same children each day as we arrived for shot after shot. Each time David's large, questioning eyes riveted to my face. My heart ached as I tried to squelch my own hot tears welling to the surface.

This is happening to my baby!

David and Charles on their toy box

*Phyllis headed to church with Charles
and holding David*

For David's sake, I tried to be calm and smile even though my insides were in meltdown. It grieved me deeply that no matter how hard I tried, I couldn't protect my children from adversity.

Another crisis happened a few months before Monty was to complete his doctorate. Two members of his dissertation committee got into a power struggle that reversed their earlier agreement that Monty had finished his dissertation. The older committee member decided to exert his power and seniority by using Monty to punish the younger committee chairman for something unrelated to Monty. In this attempt to put Monty's chairman in his place, the senior member stated he wouldn't sign the papers acknowledging Monty's completion unless Monty solved an unsolved mathematical problem. The unsolved problem pertained to the Dunford-Pettis property, which no one had been able to solve for decades.

Monty was on a leave of absence from his previous college teaching job. This delay in graduation meant his previous college would now give his teaching position to an administrator's son instead of continuing to hold it open for Monty.

Resentment and anger exploded within me against this injustice my husband had done nothing to deserve. However—to my amazement—I watched him quietly relinquish his life's dream to the Lord when he said, "If I get this degree, it will have to come from the Lord."

Over the next several months, God miraculously gave him the insight he needed to satisfy the dissenting senior committee member. Monty completed his dissertation and degree—just later than planned. I was astonished how God resolved his dilemma and opened to him an even better job. I was frustrated that I couldn't do anything to protect my husband from this bad situation, but the experience actually encouraged and strengthened both of us in our walk of faith.

Many additional crises, accidents, and deaths happened during this two-and-a-half-year period we were at OSU. The worst was what happened to my only brother-in-law's young wife and first child. Their deaths had many repercussions on our whole extended family.

Monty's mother was in the hospital for an extended time because of her high blood pressure problems, and his father was staying by her side. We were on a school break, and since it was a critical time for their father's farm, Monty and his brother, Ronnie, decided they needed to get to Odell, Texas, to plow their father's fields. The boys and I accompanied Monty to keep the men fed while they worked the fields and so I could get the house ready for my mother-in-law's return home.

While we were at the farm in Odell, our sister-in-law, Ginger, suddenly went to the hospital 250 miles away in West Texas where she and Ronnie lived. Something had gone wrong with her pregnancy, and the baby died. Family and friends began arriving from all over just as Ginger died.

When the crying and hysteria broke out, I tried to get our two and three-year-old sons away from the erupting emotional outbursts they did not understand.

They had looked forward to having a cousin younger than themselves and couldn't comprehend why relatives they knew and loved were crying.

Someone tried to comfort them about death and dying by telling them it was sort of like going to sleep. Unfortunately, at their young age, that explanation harmed rather than helped. For many months after that, neither child wanted to go to sleep for fear that either they or another family member might not be alive in the morning. I spent hours trying to get them to relax and go to sleep, only to be awakened night after night by Charles' waking from a nightmare and getting up to check and see if we were all still alive. Then it would take me another hour to get them back to sleep again.

All this stirred my deep subconscious memories of what happened when I was a ten-year-old. My only brother died right after birth, but my mother stayed in the hospital for close to a week. Daddy and I buried my brother while Mother was still in the hospital. I didn't understand the whispered adult conversations and was terrorized by the fear my mother might also die. Being only a ten-year-old, that trauma seared a strong birth/death connection into my subconscious.

As my sons worked through their own grief by daily playing funeral games, it pulled my long-buried memories to the surface. Their innocently repeated "Let's-bury-Aunt-Ginger" game and my being awakened night after night by their nightmares triggered weeks of insomnia for me. The stress and lack of sleep began affecting my health. Monty became worried and wanted me to see a doctor, but I refused and thought I would be able to handle this problem myself.

Prior to this, I had given most problems to the Lord for Him to handle. However, now when it came to my personal physical malady, I discovered I was clinging onto control. Like a stubborn child, I wanted to handle this one all by myself.

Perhaps more in America than any other country, there is a stubborn mindset of independence and resistance against submission or being told what to do. This mindset of absolute freedom probably came with the American Revolution and has spilled over into the church. Such an independent worldview places the sovereignty of God and authority of Scripture on a shelf because we don't want God—or anything—to hinder our independence.

In my extreme independent mindset, I was balking just like a child and wasn't ready to relinquish my problem to the Lord's control. I had an attitude. *Wait just a little longer, Lord. I want to work on this one myself.* I desired to obey Christ's teachings, but I also wanted to reserve veto power over a few things. I hadn't matured enough to submit to His leadership in everything. I wanted to pick and choose when and what I obeyed.

Looking back now, it seems amusing that my pride caused me to somehow think I could do something better than my Lord Jesus Christ. However, this independent, willful female had come to a critical crossroads. I had grown enough in my faith to want to learn to willingly submit to God in everything. I knew God was trustworthy. It was evident from reading Scripture and from my experience. But I was battling over something I considered *my right.* Surely I could keep control of my own body.

Hmmm . . . Scripture states that I will know that I have come to know Jesus Christ if I keep His commandments and that anyone who says he knows the Lord but does not keep His commandments is a liar (1 John 2:3–4).

I realized that if I claimed to love the Lord my God with all my heart, soul, and mind as Scripture teaches, then my choices in life would narrow to either following God's way or being in rebellion.

My own sinful willfulness reasserted itself in my circumstances—like an uncooperative toddler stubbornly shouting, "Me do it." I had to face my independent self-reliance that was so ingrained I hadn't even noticed its presence.

Once I quietly said, "Yes, Lord, I'll do whatever You show me to do," there was a fundamental shift in how I viewed my circumstances. I immediately had more peace and joy. My muscle tension relaxed because I knew I had decided to submit to Jesus Christ's lead instead of clutching white-knuckled onto my veto power. I even took my husband's suggestion and saw a doctor.

It seemed such a small personal decision at the time, but a year later, my father took me aside and asked, "What on earth changed the independent, head-strong girl I raised? Where did she go? Is Monty beating you?" I started laughing that he would consider such a ridiculous thought, but then I recognized Daddy's concern was serious. It wasn't until this conversation with my father that I recognize how much my seemingly small decision had changed me forever.

My father was correct about one thing. I was no longer the same person even though I had made no

conscious effort to change. It was merely part of the
process of submitting to God in His activity of helping
me grow. It is a lifelong process as God keeps allowing
me to see my blind spots and areas needing growth.

Take time to be holy,
Speak oft with thy Lord;
Abide in Him always,
And feed on His Word;
Make friends of God's children,
help those who are weak;
Forgetting in nothing
His blessing to seek.

Take time to be holy,
The world rushes on;
Spend much time in secret,
With Jesus alone.
By looking to Jesus,
Like Him thou shalt be;
Thy friends in thy conduct
His likeness shall see.*

---

* "Take Time to be Holy," words by William D. Longstaff, public domain,
1882, http://www.hymntime.com.

Flashback

Whoever says "I know him"
but does not keep his commandments is a liar. . . .
whoever says he abides in him ought to walk
in the same way in which he walked.
−1 John 2:4–6

Therefore, my beloved, flee from idolatry.
−1 Corinthians 10:14

Part 2: Relinquishing Idols

During those early years of marriage and facing numerous difficulties and crises together, I watched Monty closely to see if he too was growing in his walk of faith.

At one point he was head of the mathematics department in the small liberal arts college in Arkansas that hired him after graduation. Near the end of the school year of 1974–75, he found himself without a job during a nation-wide financial downturn, coupled with sweeping college-wide layoffs and faculty freezes. One university friend with multiple degrees took a garbage-truck job to keep food on his family table. Still, Monty trusted God.

He seemed confident the Lord would provide because he believed that if we sought God and followed His direction, then God would help us where we had needs (Matthew 6:31–33), but my knees were a bit shaky at believing God alone would provide for us. I realized I had actually trusted in God *plus* the-regular-paycheck-at-the-end-of-each-month. As the summer months clicked by, I too grew to trust God to provide for us even though we had no income. We watched our large spring and summer garden generously feed the four of us as well as several other faculty families who were without income.

I was glad we had no credit card debt and always saved money to pay cash for cars and furniture. We only had the monthly mortgage payment on our house.

A few days before school started in late August, we found ourselves moving to Texas for the job the

Lord had provided—at about three times Monty's previous salary. The Texas position had been open and advertised for more than a year. We were puzzled. Why had it not been filled, especially with numerous qualified candidates searching for jobs? When we saw the page-long list of qualifications any applicant had to meet before the Texas college would consider them, we understood.

The list of qualifications appeared as if someone had written up a description of my husband in intricate detail—even to the extent of stating he had to have one year of teaching experience at a junior college and couldn't have his higher degrees from Texas schools. The Lord had provided a tailor-made job for Monty more than a year before we knew he needed one!

The day after he accepted the Texas position, our Arkansas house sold to the first of several families who had called ahead of time inquiring if we would sell it. Within a week of the job interview, we were back in Texas, house hunting and full of encouragement as we saw how the Lord in His kindness was going before us in all the details of this fast move.

Watching Monty grow as our family's spiritual leader through all the good and tough times endeared him to me. I'd grown more in love with him and grateful to God for not only bringing us together but also for lending him to me as my husband during this earthly life.

Our confidence in the Lord grew like a muscle that must meet resistance to grow and stay healthy. Our difficulties strengthened our trust in God as we chose to believe His Word rather than give in to our feelings and circumstances.

But now—eleven years into marriage and relocated to the Houston, Texas, area with first and second graders settling into a new school—I longed for my life to return to smooth sailing and a sense of normalcy.

Dr. Wells, the biology professor at the previous college, had encouraged Monty to attend a particular international conference in the fall of 1975. Although we moved to Texas three days before school started in August, Monty still planned to attend.

As the day approached for his departure for the fall conference, I began feeling intense uneasiness about his trip. Once he left, my fear and apprehension soared. This had never happened to me before. What was my problem? I tried to shrug it off and busy myself with the activities of setting up our household following the move.

However, the day after he departed, everything I did to distract myself, whether by radio, magazines, or the mail, turned into an encounter describing a tragic death. Finally, in a desperate attempt to get my mind off my anxiety, I picked up a humorous book I had started reading. Within a few pages, it also began describing a terrible accident and death. Alarm bells began ringing in my mind. I knew in Scripture that Jesus said the indwelling Holy Spirit in believers both convicts and warns. Was I being warned about something?

Why had I fallen into the trap of thinking God is doing His job only when He keeps me from pain and disappointment?

If the loss of X ruined my trust in the goodness of God, it would be a signal that X had become an idol that was more important to me than God. I needed to examine this X—whether my husband, children, job, political party, money, power—no matter what or who. Did I have an idol? Not some fat little statue, but *anything* taking a higher priority in my heart over God, that is, whatever gets between God and me in our relationship.

I knew Scripture repeatedly teaches that God does not tolerate idolatry of any kind, and there are serious consequences to disobeying. Although God gives us the privilege of choice, how I use those choices can certainly get me into a lot of trouble, just as it did Eve. A pastor once said, "God gives you the sacred gift of the privilege of choice, but God does *not* give you the freedom of determining a *different outcome* to what your choice will produce." So I was agonizing and wrestling with the Lord in my spirit. I sensed that if I insisted on holding tight to my loved ones as I was doing, there would be a terrible outcome—and I might lose Monty.

I knew the Bible story about Jesus' allowing his friend Lazarus to die and the two sisters to go through days of suffering. Jesus didn't prevent the death and suffering because he had something better for them. Their brief suffering allowed Jesus to reveal an eternal truth about who he, Jesus, was when he subsequently brought Lazarus back to life. But I didn't want to think about anyone's death—not even Lazarus's.

I did find it comforting to know that Monty personally knew Christ as his Savior. He was God's child. Furthermore, I reasoned, if God is big enough to create the world and all in it, He certainly is big enough to care for His children. So I had confidence

I could trust God to give me the strength to endure whatever problem came. He would use it for our ultimate good within His perfect plan, even if it was painful. But again, how much did I really trust God? Talk is cheap, and trust is a big issue. I continued wrestling, white knuckled again. I wanted to call the shots and be in control regarding my loved ones.

Have my loved ones actually become idols to me? Surely not! Don't I just have loving concern?

I tried to rationalize and defend myself as I faced this looming choice between trusting God totally in everything—or not. I had struggled with yieldedness before, but then it had centered on my submission to God with regard to me. This was somehow new. This was an unreserved handing over of everything and everyone to Christ—even my loved ones whom I tended to tell the Lord how to protect. I was being asked to simply abide in Christ, trusting Him totally and resting in His love.

In tears, I finally relinquished those I was trying to hold onto. Instantly, I felt peace flooding me. In my mind, since I had been fighting such a sense of foreboding, I figured we had just avoided a terrible catastrophe because I relinquished everyone into the hands of the Lord to do as He saw fit. I made a mental note of the time and day this took place, never dreaming of the effects of this decision in the years ahead.

When Monty arrived home from his conference trip, I met him at the door, bombarding him with questions about what he was doing at a particular time on a specific day. He explained it was the day he had a few hours free at the conference, so he and another man hopped on a tour bus to see a few sights. However, the bus broke down during the tour, and the two men decided they shouldn't wait for its repair. They hiked several miles back to the conference center and decided to forget sightseeing.

That's it! I thought. *They were about to have something terrible happen to them, and God had protected them!*

Elated and thinking we had avoided a tragedy, I dismissed the whole episode from my mind. But several weeks later, I stood beside our wrecked car—looking at my husband—wondering if he was dead. Instantly I understand I would have gone all to pieces if the Lord hadn't prepared me ahead of time. Instead, God's peace and serenity surrounded and permeated me.

I was so thankful I had already fought this battle.

I looked at Monty—motionless and covered with blood—and knew within every fiber of my being that *he is God's child. And God is responsible for his welfare as well as for mine.* I had already settled the question of whether God is real and trustworthy. That's why I automatically took both boys into my arms and calmly told them, "Your Daddy's in the Lord's hands, and all we can do is pray." It was also why I had the déjà vu feeling as if I had already rehearsed the whole scene and knew what to do.

> *Like a River glorious, is God's perfect peace,*
> *Over all victorious, in its bright increase;*
> *Perfect, yet it floweth, fuller every day,*
> *Perfect, yet it groweth, deeper all the way.*

> [Refrain]
> *Stayed upon Jehovah, hearts are fully blest*
> *Finding, as He promised, perfect peace and*
> *rest.*[*]

---

[*]   "Like a River Glorious," words by Frances Ridley Havergal, public domain, 1876, (the words first appeared in Hymns of Consecration and Faith), http://www.hymntime.com.

CHAPTER 3

First Ambulance Ride

God is our refuge and strength,
a very present help in trouble.
−PSALM 46:1

When the Jaws of Life team arrived on the scene of our wreck with their equipment, I was unfamiliar with what they represented. I didn't know they had several types of hydraulic tools to pry trapped victims out of smashed vehicles when seconds were crucial. In utter astonishment, I watched as the men on the team cut through metal and other vehicle materials as if they were cutting through a tin can. They snapped the door post on the car like a twig in a few seconds. Then they inserted something against the door frame that enabled them to raise the dashboard and other parts of the vehicle encasing Monty. They worked diligently, lifting and bending metal to create enough clearance to free him from the metal encasing him. Then they gently slipped him out of the wreckage onto the ground. Their work was done, and they left.

Driver's seat after Jaws of Life pried it opened

Monty lay unconscious on the frozen ground, shivering and convulsing from cold and shock. Thoughtful strangers covered him with blankets from their cars, and someone slipped a pillow under his head.

While the Jaws of Life team worked to get Monty out of our vehicle, ambulances removed the three men from the truck that hit us. Then a policeman told me all the ambulances had broken down and one couldn't be found for my husband. Various people offered to load him into their car to drive all of us to a hospital, but I said we would wait for an ambulance.

I didn't want to risk puncturing or breaking something else if we tried to stuff him into a car without knowing his present injuries. Everything seemed in slow motion. Somehow time stood still or slowed down. And I was on the outside watching what was happening.

Lord, I know You're in charge of this mess. Please bring an ambulance for us.

Providentially, a young girl who looked about high school age drove up in an empty ambulance with no attendant. Some men gently loaded Monty. I slowly and painfully clambered in beside him. The friendly couple who had helped with Charles and David during this time offered to follow along behind the ambulance. They wanted to bring both boys to the hospital in their comfortable heated car.

Wow, such kind and thoughtful strangers!

As we headed toward the McCurtain County Hospital, the young lady driving the ambulance was on her walkie talkie, explaining all the red lights flashing on her dashboard. I overheard her saying, "My . . . is going out, and now . . . is also going out."

I didn't understand what she was saying because I was too busy praying. *O Lord, I don't care what you do with this ambulance, just keep it going long enough to get us to the hospital. Please, Lord!*

We actually made it to the small local hospital, which seemed a miracle in itself because the ambulance had to be towed away.

Much later during a quiet moment, I realized with gratitude how compassionate God had been. Not only did He arrange an ambulance for Monty, but He also had one of the only new Jaws of Life-trained teams nearby. He had kind locals surround us with their car lights in the darkness, and He had caring people furnish the various things we needed. He even provided the kind couple to care for two little boys suddenly in the middle of a horrific wreck.

Lord, forgive me for being so concerned about getting Monty to medical help that I almost overlooked all the love and mercy being poured out on us by you and those you brought to help.

What a friend we have in Jesus,
All our sins and griefs to bear!
What a privilege to carry
Everything to God in prayer!
O what peace we often forfeit,
O what needless pain we bear,
All because we do not carry
Everything to God in prayer.

Have we trials and temptations?
Is there trouble anywhere?
We should never be discouraged;
Take it to the Lord in prayer.
Can we find a friend so faithful,
Who will all our sorrows share?
Jesus knows our every weakness;
Take it to the Lord in prayer.*

---

*   "What a Friend We Have in Jesus," words by Joseph M. Scriven, public domain, 1855, http://www.hymntime.com.

CHAPTER 4

Second Ambulance Ride

In peace I will both lie down and sleep;
for you alone, O LORD, make me dwell in safety.
−Psalm 4:8

The small Idabell McCurtain County Hospital had achieved semi-organized bedlam with seven people from the wreck deposited in their small emergency room. The three men from the truck had been brought in earlier. The driver was now dead, but the other two men survived. Monty's injuries were so severe he could only be stabilized while we waited to be transported to a larger hospital. My sons and I were the only walking survivors of the wreck, so we shuttled back and forth between examinations by the doctors and the sheet-draped gurneys with the remaining men on them.

We were in rural Oklahoma, near the corner where southeastern Oklahoma meets Arkansas and Texas with Louisiana just southeast of that. You might think it would be easy to find another ambulance to take us to a larger hospital, but this was the beginning of the 1975 Thanksgiving holiday, and all available ambulances in the four-state area were either busy or broken down. None of the hospital personnel could find an ambulance to take us to a larger hospital. This was definitely a problem.

As the hours passed, I prayed. *Lord, You know where we're supposed to go. Please bring to the mind of one of these people someone they can contact to come get us.*

I was talking with the X-ray technician when he mentioned knowing a man in Paris, Texas, who drove an ambulance. I eagerly asked him to call on our behalf to see if he would come get us since all their existing methods had failed, and now it was late in the evening. When the X-ray technician reached the ambulance driver in Paris, he was getting ready to go to bed after a long day on the job. Miraculously, he agreed to drive the hour it would take to come to Idabel, Oklahoma, and return with us to the hospital in Paris, Texas.

When the ambulance driver arrived, he waited for the police to locate our towed vehicle, now in a junkyard in Broken Bow, Oklahoma, and gather our suitcases to take with us. He took all four of us and our luggage in his ambulance for the hour drive to Paris, Texas. He not only got us to the McCuistion Regional Medical Center but even stayed with my sons while I filled out the paperwork to get Monty checked in and eventually into a room.

Monty had been stabilized at the first hospital and talked to me periodically as I discussed various things with him. He helped me make some of the decisions, yet I later discovered he had absolutely no memory of anything we said or did. His memory skipped from the moment of impact on Wednesday to waking up on Thanksgiving Day in the Paris hospital.

Once I felt reassured that the Paris hospital was adequately taking care of Monty that night, the ambulance driver took the boys and me to a motel within walking distance of the hospital. He explained our situation to the motel owner and then helped us settle into our new location before leaving to start his next shift of work in a few hours. God bless that man! He was an overflowing answer to prayer.

Exhausted, the boys and I settled down to get a few hours of sleep before morning. With lights off, I was trying to quiet my racing thoughts when a little voice called out in the darkness, "Mom, if Daddy dies, are you going to remarry?"

Stunned, I blurted out, "Good grief, *no!* Besides, your daddy's not going to die! . . . Anyway, not now! We'll all make it through this. You need to go to sleep. Your grandparents are arriving tomorrow, and we'll have a busy day."

Exhausted and desperately wanting to catch a few hours of sleep myself, this son's question sent my mind whirling with questions of my own.

Where did that question come from? What did the boys see after the wreck? Did they see the dead driver and his two passengers out on the highway? I know they saw all of them in the hospital. What did the strangers trying to distract and watch over the boys tell them about all this? Did this bring back to the boys' minds the chaos of when their aunt and her baby died several years ago? Okay, Phyllis, take a deep breath. Let's deal with what you can do and not fret about what you can't change.

Lord, thanks for protecting and enabling the three of us to walk away from the wreck. They're only six and seven years old and unfortunately have seen a lot more tragedy than multitudes of adults. I know they thought their dad was dead at first, so they've undoubtedly been traumatized. And I probably haven't been as sensitive to their needs as I could have been. Please heal their emotions and memories of whatever they have been exposed to tonight. And, Lord, please help Monty rest and get whatever help he needs.

Lord, thank You for being with us through all of this. I feel that I'm going through a valley of the shadow of death, but I genuinely sense that You are with me and comforting me—just as You promised.*

Go with our parents as they try to get here. They're so distraught. Please watch over them and protect them as they drive. We certainly don't need any more wrecks right now. Amen.

The LORD is my Shepherd; I shall not want.
He makes me to lie down in green pastures.
He leads me beside still waters.

He restores my soul. He leads me
in paths of righteousness
for His Name's sake.

*Even though I walk through the valley,
of the shadow of death,
I will fear no evil, for you are with me;
your rod and your staff, they comfort me.

You prepare a table before me
in the presence of my enemies;
you anoint my head with oil;
my cup overflows.

Surely goodness and mercy shall follow me
all the days of my life,
and I shall dwell in the house of the LORD
forever.

—PSALM 23:1–6

CHAPTER 5

Revisiting the Wrecked Vehicle

For he will command his angels concerning you
to guard you in all your ways.
—PSALM **91:11**

When I arrived at Monty's room the next morning, I was horrified to find his face and upper body still covered with blood.

"Why hasn't he been cleaned up?" I hissed to a nurse.

She assured me he had been cleaned up. It was their hospital policy to not scrub the blood off because it was the first scab. They had discovered there was less scarring if the blood is left as the first scab on the wounds.

His face, left arm, and upper chest had been bombarded with shattered glass from the windshield and side window. The glass was so embedded in his skin that small pieces worked their way to the surface for years afterward. And just as the hospital staff predicted, Monty ended up with almost no scarring on his face and upper torso.

After I adjusted to the fact he was still covered in blood, I began looking at all the wires and pulleys attaching both his legs and the lower part of his body to the ceiling. I shuddered each time I looked at the metal rods through his ankles and legs that connected to all the wires and pulleys. He was in traction because his left leg was broken just below the hip. They were using traction to hold things stable while waiting for the swelling to go down so they could perform surgery in about a week.

Soon his parents arrived from Odell, Texas. I tried to stop them outside his room to explain why he was so bloody. His mom shoved right past me and dashed into the room. She screamed and almost fainted. It certainly wasn't good for her high blood pressure.

However, when my parents arrived from Kansas, they were more prepared for the sight. My dad had put himself through college by driving an ambulance at night and had seen multiple wrecks.

Daddy insisted on driving back to Oklahoma to see our wrecked car. I needed to get a copy of the police report of the accident for the insurance company. We would do it all in one trip. One of the nurses produced a polaroid camera and suggested I take pictures of the wrecked vehicle to show Monty. She said it would help him understand the day missing in his memory.

The boys and I rode with Daddy on the hour-long drive. When we arrived at the Deadman's Curve where the wreck occurred, he pulled off the highway to examine where our car landed after being hit. The boys tumbled out to scout for any Legos left behind or small pieces of the wreckage left as souvenirs.

As we looked around, I understood how the highway construction plan—to straighten out the curve—had figured into the logistics of our wreck. The truck was approaching the curve on the newer four-lane straightaway part of the road. The driver was using that mile or more straightaway to test drive how fast his newly replaced truck motor would go. We had been approaching from the other side of the curve where the old two-lane road had not yet been straightened and widened. The highway construction along the side of the old road was a maze of concrete with metal reinforcing rods sticking vertically into the air—just a few feet from where we landed. My pulse quickened as I realized we had landed on about the only relatively safe and level spot in the whole construction site where we would not be impaled by the reinforcing rods.

Thank you, Lord. You guided our landing spot.

We located the junkyard where our vehicle had been taken, and I took pictures with the borrowed Polaroid camera. I have been grateful ever since to have had the privilege of revisiting the site and having photos of the vehicle to show Monty and others. They remind us of how bad the car looked and how blessed we were to all still be alive.

Daddy walked around and around our heavy Mercury Marquis station wagon and wept. He kept saying, "I can't believe anyone came out of this vehicle alive. I've scooped up pieces of people who were in a much less severe wreck. Honey, God had to be protecting you because humanly, no one should have come out of this alive, much less all four of you."

He pointed out that our gas tank had been clipped as the approaching truck disintegrated from the impact and parts of the pickup came over and down the side of us. He pointed out that a front-end wreck at a combined force of at least 150 miles an hour, with a full gas tank, should have ignited. We had just stopped to get gas, and I well remembered the smell of gasoline that had spilled out.

"It should have caught fire, Phyllis!" He shook his head and repeated again, "It had to be a miracle that there was not an explosion or fire."

As what he said sank in, I shuddered at the thought of Monty being encased in a metal cocoon if the car had caught fire. Then I remembered two men walked around the vehicle after the accident marveling at how our vehicle had not burned. They had warned people to make sure there were no cigarettes anywhere near.

Thank you, Lord, for not even letting me be aware of this possibility until now. And thank you for the two men warning people.

*Blurry old picture taken with borrowed camera
shows author's father, Buel Smith, and her sons
with their car at the junk yard*

Another old picture of our wrecked car in 1975

As I looked at our wrecked car from a new perspective, I remembered seeing the approaching truck driver frantically trying to steer back toward his lane just before the time of impact. As he did, the headlight in front of me began to rise for his truck began to tilt—causing Monty's side of our vehicle to take more of the impact than my side. *That's probably what saved my life.* However, that meant the truck not only smashed the front of our car in on us, but part of it went above and down the driver's side of our vehicle before coming to a stop.

While Daddy waited, I crawled back into our wrecked car one last time to collect remaining toys, more belongings, and my parents' Christmas presents. Behind the driver's seat, I found something strange. It looked like a chunk of dried bacon. Puzzled, I picked it up and commented to Daddy about it. He immediately recognized it as the dried flesh gouged out of Monty's neck. The gouge had just grazed his jugular vein.

As I held the large walnut-sized chunk of dried flesh in my hand, I recognized that Monty was only a fraction of an inch from having his jugular vein cut and bleeding to death while trapped. I was overwhelmed with gratitude as I grasped how our loving heavenly Father had intervened in so many large and small details. His hand guided the hood to fold right at Monty's forehead and now this.

God, in His rich mercy, is always there and doing more than we realize.

Great is thy faithfulness, O God my Father;
There is no shadow of turning with Thee;
Thou changest not, Thy compassions, they fail
not;
As Thou has been, Thou forever wilt be.

[Refrain]
Great is Thy faithfulness!
Great is Thy faithfulness!
Morning by morning new mercies I see.
All I have needed Thy hand hath provided;
Great is Thy faithfulness, Lord, unto me!

---

* "Great is thy Faithfulness," words by Thomas O. Chisholm, public domain, 1923, http://www.hymntime.com.

CHAPTER 6

Quick Trip Home

On the day I called, you answered me;
my strength of soul you increased.
—PSALM 138:3

The following days were filled with tests as doctors tried to determine the extent of my husband's injuries. They did plastic surgery to fill the gaping hole gouged in his neck. We feared the worst of a lot of things, especially regarding all the head and chest injuries. But every test revealed promising results. It was as if God had His hands around Monty and would allow only so much damage.

The doctors decided to wait a week before scheduling surgery on his broken leg. They wanted time for the swelling to subside. The steering wheel had broken on his chest, the steering column had dropped between his legs, and all of his body had been severely battered as the front, side, and top of the car came in on him. This delay meant I could drive the 350 miles across Texas to return the boys to their school after Thanksgiving and make it back before his surgery.

Monty's parents had brought us one of their cars to use until we got something to replace our demolished station wagon. I loaded the boys into the borrowed car and headed south across Texas toward Houston. I had never driven several hundred miles all at one time because Monty liked to do most of the driving. Being exhausted from the whole ordeal and still having the left side of my body in constant pain, I was not thrilled to head out on a long drive. No one warned me that it might not be safe to take such a long drive by myself after my own head injury—or if they did, I didn't listen. Everything within me wanted to stay with my husband, but logically it appeared I should drive the boys home since I didn't see how anyone else could do all that needed to be done.

There were times on the long drive home when I questioned my sanity in thinking I could make this drive. When my vision would blur and things began to swim, I pulled off the road at the rest stops to close my eyes and rest while the boys ran off their energy outside the car.

Back in the Houston suburb of Baytown, I got them settled in with a caring family who had several children attending their elementary school. I deposited them, their clothes, and school supplies at their new temporary home so they could go to school on Monday with their friends.

Since I had no idea how long it would be before I would come back home, I attempted to take care of other things I considered necessary before returning to Monty. However, the phone kept ringing every few minutes. I was truly grateful for all the love from many concerned people, but I couldn't get much done for answering their questions. In exasperation, I finally dumped everything into the car and drove north—even though it was already late in the day, and I had planned to spend the night at home. There would be no peace at home since the phone wouldn't stop ringing. Thankfully, there were no cell phones back then, or the calls would have followed me.

On the northern outskirts of Houston, exhaustion and pain overcame my will to keep going. I had to stop and sleep, even though I had only driven a few miles. I was drained. I didn't have any broken bones, but the nerve damage to the left side of my body with its accompanying aches and pain was getting to me.

It was a rather seedy roadside motel, but I needed a place to straighten out and sleep before I collapsed. In the quiet of the car, I discovered I was so emotionally and physically exhausted I felt I might pass out.

All went well in the motel until about midnight. I got so cold I woke up. The heater in the room didn't work. There were no extra blankets and no one at the front desk. I was on my own. Nothing I tried helped me feel warmer, and I couldn't stop shivering.

In that cold, half-awake, dazed state—I felt so alone. In the eleven years I'd been married, I had never traveled by myself. Monty had always been by my side when I needed him to help me or to fix things. But now I was alone, so very alone. Monty was a long drive across Texas in a hospital, and our two young sons were behind me in the home of new friends for who knew how long. My parents had returned to Kansas, and Monty's family had returned to West Texas. I was tired, achy, and sleepy. Never had I felt so alone, vulnerable, and distraught.

I couldn't stop shivering. My teeth were chattering so hard I wondered if I might chip one. In desperation, I grabbed everything and moved back into the car— at least the car had a heater to warm me.

Mmm, the heat feels wonderful! Guess I'll head north, even though it's two in the morning. So I started driving.

I stopped at a red light on I 45 in the north part of Houston, and the car went dead. I couldn't restart it. Trying not to panic, I glanced over my right shoulder and noticed the only light visible was from an all-night gas station down a side ramp behind me.

"Okay, Lord, please help me coast backward off this freeway into that gas station that's still open. This is not a good place to be stranded."

I held my breath as I changed gears and waited.

"Here goes."

The car began rolling backward.

I slowly and successfully coasted to a stop in the driveway of the gas station. The young attendant came out to check on me. With my window rolled down a bit to keep in my warm air, I described what had happened to the car.

"No problem, lady. My dad has a car like this, and it does the same thing. I'll stay with you and direct you through this until you get it started."

And he did!

Shortly, I was on the road again and encouraged that God was definitely going with me. Driving through the dark early morning with all the truckers,

I sensed a strange bubbly sense of joy and gratitude pouring out of my heart. If I tried to suppress it, I felt I would explode. So I expressed my emotions by singing. *This is good,* I thought. *It'll keep me awake.*

After a while, it began dawning on me that these were not lyrics or melodies I knew. Somehow I was making them up on the fly. For hours, continuous songs of joy, thanksgiving, and praise poured forth out of me—words and music I hadn't learned. However, they seemed so perfect for the moment. Somewhere in the back of my mind, I kept listening and wishing I could write down these words and music. They were beautiful beyond anything I remembered ever hearing. I was strengthened, and my spirit was revived.

God's hand not only ministered to my physical needs, but His Spirit also uplifted my spirit.

In the early hours of that bleak November morning, a few truckers might have thought I seemed out of place as they gazed down on the young woman singing her heart out as she rolled along the highway with them. But I was at peace. At that moment in time, I had never been happier or more grateful to God for all his love and grace.

Earlier in the night, I felt so alone to be facing all the uncertainty ahead, but now I recognized I was not alone. Regardless of my own physical condition, I could make this long drive and confidently face whatever the future might hold. Although the *love of my life* was suspended in traction from the ceiling of a distant hospital, the *Lover of my soul* was here with me—right now—on this journey.

The truest joy does not come through circumstances but through Him who is with us in our circumstances.

> *There's within my heart a melody*
> *Jesus whispers sweet and low,*
> *Fear not, I am with thee, peace, be still,*
> *In life's constant ebb and flow.*

> [Refrain]
> *Jesus, Jesus, Jesus,*
> *Sweetest Name I know,*
> *Fills my ev'ry longing,*
> *Keeps me singing as I go.**

---

* "He Keeps Me Singing," words by Luther B. Bridgers, public domain, (in The Revival No. 6, by Charles D. Tillman [Atlanta, Georgia: 1910], number 21, alt.), http://www.hymntime.com.

More Car Trouble

You keep him in perfect peace
whose mind is stayed on you,
because he trusts in you.
—Isaiah **26:3**

S hortly after the sun came up, I exited the freeway and parted ways with the big-rig truckers. Now it was two-lane roads winding through east Texas pastures and farm country. Having just passed through a small rural town, I estimated I was about an hour from Paris, where Monty would be waiting. We hadn't talked since I left the Houston area the previous day, so he would be getting anxious about my arrival.

"Oh no!" *There's a red light flashing on my dashboard! Now what? I'm miles from anywhere, and I don't see any farmhouses where I might find a phone.*

There's a wide spot. Guess I'll stop. Don't want to damage my father-in-law's car.

As I pulled off the road, a man in a pickup passed by. He slowed and made a U-turn.

Fear seized my heart. *A woman alone. Beside the highway. What if he has evil intent? Lord, help me.*

He swung his pickup around and pulled up on my right side. I hesitated as my hand touched the door handle. Suddenly I sensed a voice saying, *"After all I've done for you, and you doubt Me now?"*

I jumped out of the car, invigorated by the realization that God was still in control. The middle-aged man and I lifted the hood. After checking several things, he determined the problem was beyond his knowledge. Climbing back into his pickup, he shouted over his shoulder, "I'll go back to the last town and find a mechanic to help you."

As he swung around to go back to the last town, believe it or not, the mechanic from the last town pulled in on the other side of my car—in his tow truck. The mechanic quickly decided he could get the unique part I needed in the larger town where he just happened to be headed. He would then come back to tow my vehicle to his shop and fix it.

As the three of us stood around the car discussing the problem, I mentioned I was headed to the Paris hospital, where my husband was a patient. The first driver in the truck just happened to be driving through Paris on his way to see an aunt he visited twice a year. He kept saying that for some unknown reason he was running a little late this year, but he would be glad to drop me off at the hospital so my husband wouldn't be worried about me.

I grabbed my suitcase, hopped into the pickup with one stranger, and left a borrowed car with another stranger who promised to fix it. I felt totally at peace. God was in control, and this was fine.

As I bounced along in the truck with my good Samaritan, it turned out he had once broken his leg in much the same place as Monty. He too had been faced with similar choices about what to do, and doctors had put a metal rod in his leg. I was shocked because he seemed to walk fine, and I was delighted! I was not excited because he had broken his leg, but because he was someone who could answer some of our questions. Monty and I were only in our thirties and didn't know anyone who had a rod in their leg. We were desperately wishing to talk to someone who had personal experience. This was before internet

and Google searches, so we were quite perplexed and
had lots of questions.

"Would it be asking too much of you to go with
me to Monty's room? He has lots of questions and
needs to see that you can still walk around normally
and—"

"Sure, I can do that. It won't take long."

I hesitated, and then timidly continued, "He may
want to know if you can still do squats or whatever
those man-things are that men seem to think they
must still be able to do—just in case they decide to
put shingles on their roof or some such thing."

He laughed heartily. "Okay."

I sighed in relief as his laughter washed over me. It
felt refreshing and somehow freeing to hear someone
laugh again. On top of the privilege of having a
ride to the hospital, God provided exactly the right
person to bless my husband in this unexpected way.

In Monty's hospital room our new friend
explained and demonstrated the impact of having a
metal rod in his leg. Then he was out the door to
continue his biannual trip to his aunt's house.

*Hmmm . . . now I know why I had to wake up in
the middle of the night to drive across Texas. Lord, I'm
so ashamed I grumbled. You wanted me to be in just
the right place to meet both of my good Samaritans at*

the exact moment all three of our paths could cross—so one of them would answer all the questions Monty and I were praying for someone to answer.

Please bless those two men and others like them whom You use to bless and help Your people. You have such a loving heart, Lord. You are with me in all these various situations and keep finding ways to show your love. How so like You to use what I thought were problems to get me in the correct place for a special blessing and answered prayer.

What a fellowship, what a joy divine,
Leaning on the everlasting arms;
What a blessedness, what a peace is mine,
Leaning on the everlasting arms.

[Refrain]
Leaning, leaning,
Safe and secure from all alarms;
Leaning, leaning,
*Leaning on the everlasting arms.**

---

* "Leaning on the Everlasting Arms," words by Elisha A. Hoffman, public domain, (in The Glad Evangel [Dalton, Georgia: A. J. Showalter, 1887]), http://www.hymntime.com.

CHAPTER 8

Another Good Samaritan

Your Father knows what you need
before you ask him.
—MATTHEW 6:8

After the pickup truck driver left the hospital room, Monty and I tried to catch up on what had been happening during the last couple of days. In my haste to reach the hospital that morning, I hadn't eaten breakfast. Now my hunger pains couldn't be ignored. I headed across the room to go eat in the cafeteria, and Monty's phone rang just as I reached the door. I paused with my hand on the door handle.

"Yes, this is Monty Kester." Then he listened in silence, wrote something down, and smiled.

"Thank you. I appreciate your help. My wife will be out to get the car soon."

"What?" I exclaimed in disbelief as I heard what he promised.

Our eyes met, but neither of us said a word—eyes and expressions can do a lot of talking. The unspoken question hanging in the air was, "How on earth was I going to get the car that was an hour away?"

Somehow, in all my haste and anticipation of seeing him again, this problem hadn't entered my mind.

I stared at him, too stunned to say anything and startled that he promised I would get the car soon. We were interrupted by someone knocking on the door my hand was still clutching.

"Hi there, we're from the local First Baptist Church and heard about your wreck. We thought we would drop by to see if there's anything we could do to help you folks."

Is this for real? Regaining my composure, I responded, "How sweet of you," as I swung the door open for the entrance of the two men. "Won't you come in?"

Monty grabbed the hand bar above his bed to pull himself as upright as possible since most of his body was in traction. He smiled at the two newcomers and responded, "Yes, there certainly is something you can do for us. My wife is driving a borrowed car that broke down as she was driving back from south Texas, and I just got a phone call telling me it's fixed. She needs a way to go pick it up about an hour south of here. Could you gentlemen help her get the car?"

The more elderly of our visitors smiled. "Sure, Mr. Kester. I'll be glad to take her to pick up the car. Just give me about an hour to go get my young grandson, and I'll be back to take her."

We all agreed and worked out the details. I even had time to eat before leaving. Soon I returned to Paris in the newly fixed car.

Every time I entered Monty's room the cables and pulleys suspending him from the ceiling reminded me that he couldn't go anywhere or do anything as he waited in traction for the swelling to go down enough to have surgery. He had helplessly waited as I took off in a borrowed car to drive 700 miles round trip to Houston. Then this morning he was jolted to see me return with one stranger and later go out the door with another stranger to a destination unknown to Monty.

Yet once our elderly helper mentioned he would go get his young grandson before returning for me, Monty smiled. The tension left his face, and he leaned back against his pillows with a peaceful look. It was the Lord putting a nice bow on top of his endless package of provision.

Not only did God move those two men to decide to visit us before we knew we needed help, He even took care of a detail like Monty's peace of mind and his confidence in the intentions of a stranger. Can you think of a better illustration of God's tender lovingkindness saturating His knowledge of all things?

Be not dismayed whate'er betide,
God will take care of you;
Beneath His wings of love abide,
God will take care of you

[Refrain]
God will take care of you,
Through every day, o'er all the way;
He will care for you,
God will take care of you.

---

* "God Will Take Care of You," words by Civilla D. Martin, public domain, 1904 (first appeared in Songs of Redemption and Praise, by John A. Davis, 1905), http://www.hymntime.com.

CHAPTER 9

The Second Hospital

And we know that for those who love God
all things work together for good,
for those who are called according to his purpose.
−ROMANS 8:28

I n the beginning when we arrived at McCuistion Regional Medical Center in Paris, I called our surgeon friend, Dr. Jim Strangemeir in Baytown, a suburb of Houston. I wanted Jim to help me explore getting Monty across Texas to a Houston hospital. I figured Houston was bigger and had to be a better place medically for Monty. After finding out where we were and the doctors who were seeing Monty, Jim assured me we should stay where we were. So I gave up trying to move him to Houston and settled down to the hope that maybe we could make it back home before Christmas to be with our sons.

The day Monty was scheduled for surgery, the nurses repeatedly tried to prepare me for what he would be like afterwards. Apparently, having a metal rod shoved through your hip and down through the center of a bone causes excruciating pain.

Later, when they were preparing him to stand and take a few steps after the surgery, I was again asked if I was sure I wanted to stay in the room.

"Mrs. Kester, I really don't think you want to be in this room when we get him up on his feet. He'll use words you didn't know he knew. In fact, if he's like other patients, he'll turn the air blue with cursing. You might prefer to wait outside until this is over."

No one was going to chase me out of his room. All their words of warning strengthened my resolve that it was important that I remain with him. I was as steeled for this as he was. I pressed my back against a wall and held my breath as the young woman fastened straps around him and asked him to stand up.

He did.

And he did not make a sound.

She asked him if he thought he could walk to the end of the bed.

He nodded. Then he motioned to the door.

"Are you wanting to walk across the room to the door?" she asked in disbelief.

He nodded.

I watched with bated breath as he slowly walked to the end of the bed, across the room, and then returned with the amazed woman in tow with her straps attached to his waist. They looked useless to me. But what do I know? Yet he made about two of her in size, and I didn't see how she had a prayer of holding him up if he started to fall.

He never uttered a sound the whole time. Still, I recognized that clenched jaw. I had seen that before and would see it again and again as he dealt with severe pain. However, cursing or using the Lord's name in vain was not part of his rehabilitation process.

As the week progressed, every person who entered his room complimented him about the great walk he took his first time out of bed. Even the cleaning lady and the fellow washing and shaving him knew about it.

It was then I connected the dots regarding things I had been hearing and noticing about this second hospital. Daily, when I went downstairs to eat in the cafeteria, I kept meeting and eating with people who praised this medical center. On several occasions when I was eating, I asked someone I met how their loved one ended up at this particular hospital. Several mentioned that their loved one had been told in another hospital that there was nothing that could be done for them or that they were simply going to die. In each case, the person I talked to had managed to get their loved one transferred to this medical center, and sure enough they were getting better.

It was beginning to make sense. No place is perfect, but I don't think we could have had a more caring staff anywhere. Nor could we have found a place with better lines of communication throughout their entire team. It seemed every improvement Monty made was praised by each staff member as they came to his room—even the lady cleaning the floor. This was repeated over and over all the weeks until we left for home.

I wonder. . . . Could it be that my loving heavenly Father caused all the ambulances to break down or be busy in a four-state area just as we needed one after getting to the first hospital? This apparent ambulance problem forced us to be taken to the best possible place we could be for Monty's particular injuries. It's happening again! What I originally thought was a terrible problem actually turned out to be a blessing in disguise. I prayed in the emergency room of that first hospital for God to get us to wherever He thought would be best for us. He certainly answered that prayer.

I'm beginning to feel loved in a special way that is stretching my concept of God. Not only is He with me, but He seems to be way ahead of me on all sorts of details as I go through all this. It seems He really does love me . . . and with a tenderness I never expected.

God moves in a mysterious way
His wonders to perform;
He plants his footsteps in the sea,
And rides upon the storm.

Ye fearful saints, fresh courage take;
The clouds ye so much dread
Are big with mercy and shall break
In blessings on your head.

His purposes will ripen fast,
Unfolding every hour;
The bud may have a bitter taste,
But sweet will be the flower.

Blind unbelief is sure to err,
And scan His work in vain.
God is His own interpreter,
*And He will make it plain.**

---

* "God Moves in a Mysterious Way," words by William Cowper, public domain (in Twenty-Six Letters on Religious Subjects, by John Newton, 1774), http://www.hymntime.com.

CHAPTER 10

Housing and Use
of Spare Time

*And my God will supply every need of yours
according to his riches in glory in Christ Jesus.*
—PHILIPPIANS 4:19

When I had driven the boys back to Houston so they could return to school after Thanksgiving, I knew I needed to find some things to occupy Monty and myself during all the weeks we would be in Paris. Monty's doctors had sounded like he would be at the hospital until, and possibly beyond, Christmas. That left several things to weigh heavily on my mind.

One primary concern was about Monty having something to occupy his mind during his weeks in the hospital. At the age of thirty-five, he was not one to be satisfied with just talking, playing games, or watching TV. And this was before smart phones and personal computers. His restless, inquiring mind needed something to challenge it even though his body was restricted. I eventually selected several of his books and a small suitcase he had filled with cassette tapes on systematic theology, along with a portable cassette player.

Another concern was the cost and location of a suitable motel room for me to rent continuously for all the weeks I would accompany Monty in Paris.

He had graduated from a small West Texas farm community high school with eight in his graduating class. In fact, Odell's school was so small they closed it down after he graduated and consolidated with another school. During the two days I was away from Monty while I drove the boys home, a lot happened regarding our needs and that small Texas high school.

Since our wreck had only been a few minutes after 6 p.m. on the first day of the Thanksgiving holiday season, it was heralded as the first fatality wreck for Thanksgiving 1975. Information about it —and apparently about us—was carried over various news outlets across the land, as evidenced by cards and calls from around the country. Monty's parents had to tell at least one person in Odell because they arranged for someone to care for their horses and cows when they drove across Texas to bring us a car and to see Monty in the Paris hospital.

Of course, telling one person in a small town usually means that everyone will soon know. So it was not surprising that one of Monty's former high school classmates contacted him. The surprising thing was that out of all the places he could have lived, it was just a few miles from the hospital where Monty was being treated. He and his wife invited me to stay in their guest room for as long as I needed to be in Paris.

Hmmm . . . I think I'm seeing the handiwork of the Lord again.

It turned out this friend's wife was in a difficult place in her own life. So during several days she and I talked late into the evenings after I left the hospital. She even had a large hardcover book that a cult was pushing her to read and follow. Since she knew and trusted Monty, she asked him to read the book and advise her about the beliefs described in it.

Wow! Both of our needs were met in one household.

I was surprised that God not only supplied our needs but also used and stretched both of us in

the process! I shouldn't have been surprised. Over
time, I'd been discovering I couldn't get through
a day without talking and praying to the Lord
about whatever was going on. He is a dear friend,
and you talk frequently with whomever you have a
close relationship. When something weighs heavily
on my heart and mind, He knows my needs better
than I do and is able to provide in ways I don't even
know about. Not only did I have a nice place to stay,
but Monty also had something to fully challenge
and occupy his mind the entire time he was in the
hospital and for some time afterwards.

Some evenings as dusk approached, he would
suggest I head home early before it got dark.
Then with a smile, he would wink and add that
it would give me some time to visit with her and
him more time to work on his task of reading the
entire cult book for her. Eventually he wrote her
a letter explaining in detail how three basic topics
in the book were not biblically based. In fact, his
research, studying, and systematic organization of
biblical knowledge eventually turned his letter into
a twenty-six-page paper on the biblical basis and
explanation of (1) the church, (2) salvation, and (3)
security of the believer.

Although we didn't know it at the time, the systematic organization of biblical knowledge he acquired during that time laid a solid foundation for him on other tasks that lay ahead of us over the years. No one but God knew the importance of Monty's studying and gaining foundational knowledge, and I don't know when else he would have had such a concentrated and uninterrupted time to devote to it.

As I drove back and forth to the hospital, I marveled at what the Lord was doing. He truly does supply our needs according to His riches. He genuinely loves us and knows our strengths and needs.

I would let this truth wash over me repeatedly. Not only did He give Monty a big challenge, He even took my mind off our predicament by forcing me to use the knowledge from the marriage seminar I had team-taught with Monty a few months earlier.

Lord, don't ever let me forget that we all face a series of great opportunities brilliantly disguised as problems. More and more I'm realizing how You often use what looks like a problem for my ultimate good.

He leadeth me, O blessed thought!
O words with heav'nly comfort fraught!
Whate'er I do, where'er I be,
Still 'tis God's hand that leadeth me.

[Refrain]
He leadeth me, He leadeth me,
By His own hand He leadeth me;
His faithful follower I would be,
For by His hand He leadeth me.*

---

*   "He Leadeth Me," words by Joseph H. Gilmore, public domain, 1862,
    http://www.hymntime.com.

CHAPTER 11

Getting Home

He fulfills the desire of those who fear him;
he also hears their cry and saves them.
−PSALM **145:19**

As Christmas approached, I was encouraged that both boys seemed to be thriving as they stayed with the large family. This gave them others to play with and kept them distracted. However, Monty and I missed them terribly and didn't want to be separated at Christmas time. We yearned to be back together as a family and in our own home. Monty was, of course, highly motivated to progress enough for us to return home before Christmas.

As I began exploring ways to transport him across Texas once he was released from the hospital,

I ran into difficulties. Although he was recovering rapidly, he still couldn't sit up longer than an hour or so at a time, which meant he had to be transported lying down at least part of the way. I had naively thought I could drive him home in our borrowed car, but that would not work if we were going to go home before Christmas.

This meant I had the additional problem of getting the borrowed car to south Texas since it was to be our transportation until we could get another vehicle. The expense of hiring an ambulance to get Monty to and from airports or to drive him across Texas was staggering. The costs and logistics of our options appeared impossible and out of reach for our budget.

As I researched and struggled with our dilemma, Dave—an Exxon engineer we had recently met in the church we were attending in Baytown—called Monty to discuss how we planned to get home. I was surprised Dave knew about the situation and even more astonished that out of the blue he called Monty. He told Monty he wanted to strap a twin bed in his family's van and drive to Paris so he could bring Monty home. Would that work for us?

You bet it would! It would also enable me to drive the borrowed car across Texas with them instead of all by myself. Hip, hip hooray!

My excitement grew as our plans began taking shape regarding how we would finally get to return home before Christmas. The day before we were to check out, Monty received a lovely get-well card from a group of our new Texas neighbors in Baytown. I was amazed they knew what had happened but even more surprised by the loose cash included in the card. Touched by their generosity and thoughtfulness, I dropped their card in my purse as I began collecting things for the move home.

Goodness, what sweet neighbors. Glad we got their card before we leave tomorrow.

The next day as I was checking Monty out of the hospital, I got a shock. I had been juggling all the different insurance claims concerning the accident and assumed insurance would pay for all the hospital expenses. But the hospital business office required me to pay a certain amount of cash before they released Monty. I pulled out my checkbook, but the clerk repeated that it had to be in cash, not a check or credit card. It was the weekend, and the banks were closed. Then I remembered the card in my purse from our neighbors with cash enclosed. Amazing! It paid for Monty's release from the hospital with enough left over to buy gas and meals for all three of us on the trip home. And I had been wondering why the neighbors sent cash—especially such an amount.

God coordinated all those people to collect the money and get it to us with perfect timing and abundance. His love and providence kept showing up.

I soon found that Monty's driver, Dave, was one of those gentle giants who had seemingly thought of everything to care for Monty on the trip across Texas. He drove slow enough not to jostle Monty on curvy or rough roads. The doctor had given Monty some extra medications in case he needed them for the long trip. Yet the arrangement of the bed in the van worked amazingly well. And truth be told, he and Dave had a grand time together because after weeks of talking mostly to me, Monty was delighted to talk with a man.

As I drove across Texas behind Dave's van, I had lots of time to think. I rehearsed in my mind the amazing ways God had shown His love to us through this whole episode. I found it astonishing how He kept going ahead of us and providing for our needs before we were even aware we had a problem. Not just once but over and over and over.

> *Simply trusting every day,*
> *Trusting through a stormy way;*
> *Even when my faith is small,*
> *Trusting Jesus, that is all.*

> [Refrain]
> *Trusting as the moments fly,*
> *Trusting as the days go by;*
> *Trusting Him whate'er befall,*
> *Trusting Jesus, that is all.**

---

*   "Trusting Jesus," words by Edgar Page Stites, public domain, 1876 (lyrics first appeared as a poem in a newspaper), http://www.hymntime.com.

CHAPTER 12

The New Vehicle

Delight yourself in the LORD,
and he will give you the desires of your heart.
−PSALM 37:4

Once we were home, the insurance company—of the man who hit us—called. He had been trying to find a replacement Mercury Marquis station wagon suitable for us. He checked all over the Houston area to locate the same type we had, and he found one: same color, one year newer, low mileage, and only driven one year. The insurance representative asked if he could bring the vehicle to our house so we could see it.

I was amazed. I had been so busy arranging for all the other aspects of getting home that I hadn't even thought about getting a replacement car. I figured we would get around to finding a vehicle once Monty could be up and walking around better. We assumed the insurance company would give us cash for our totaled vehicle and never dreamed they would personally try to find a replacement for us to have as soon as we got home.

When the car dealer and the insurance representative arrived at our house with the station wagon, they helped me get Monty out of the house to view the vehicle. Between all of us, we maneuvered him and his big cast into the station wagon. They explained everything and drove us around to see if we both approved of it as a replacement vehicle for our wrecked wagon. On the outside, it looked exactly like our old vehicle. In fact, several neighbors were puzzled for weeks because they thought we had wrecked our vehicle, yet they could see it sitting in our driveway—or so they thought.

Years earlier, Monty and I written a list of all we wanted in our ideal family car. It was one of those crazy things we did as a family one time as we were driving somewhere. And I saved the piece of paper. Driven by curiosity, I searched and found it. We had listed all the things we specifically wanted, and what we definitely didn't want, our ideal car to have. For example, we all wanted bench seats, and I definitely did not wish to have automatic windows. I figured automatic windows would be a pain since I would probably be driving carloads of rowdy boys who love to play with mechanical things.

As I reread our entire list, my knees grew weak, and I sank into a chair in awe. Our replacement vehicle had precisely everything we had written that we wanted or didn't want in our imaginary ideal car. Not only that, there were also extras we were not even aware were available—and I loved them. Like the lighted mirror on my passenger sun visor, and that the rear portion of the wagon could be folded into two small facing bench seats.

I later would find that the twin bench seats in the back were wonderful when hauling a load of cub scouts. The scouts all thought the benches were their special seats and scrambled into the back. That left the two large bench seats at the front for the adults and put the pack of loud, rowdy boys in the back. This vehicle served us well during all those years of driving groups of young boys to swim meets and on school or scouting excursions.

How farsighted and thoughtful for the Lord to take care of such details before I even knew my need.

And there's more. This particular vehicle had originally been bought new by a ship captain at the Port of Houston, driven by his wife for a year, and then traded for a new vehicle just before we needed it. I had never thought about God's caring about such small details—and so far in advance.

I'm staggered at the sovereign providence and faithfulness of God, who is not only the Creator of the universe but is also the Ruler of it. He who existed before the beginning of time even cares about meticulous details that affect me in my life.

In the past when I read about Jesus' life during his years on earth, I was always impressed by the way He stopped and paid attention to people along the way. He always seemed to have the time to be interrupted by children or supposedly unimportant common people. I guess that somewhere in the back of my mind, I thought His loving acts of thoughtfulness only applied to people back in Bible times and not to me and others living now.

As I kept catching glimpses of the love that God was lavishing on us during this time, I recognized how wrong I was. His love didn't only compel Jesus to take the penalty that was due me for my sinfulness, but His heart of love just won't quit giving.

My sense of being loved by God was growing stronger and stronger. Every time I drove that replacement vehicle, it reminded me of God's provision poured out on us. He knew the desires of my heart and prepared the perfect vehicle for us before we even had the wreck.

When upon life's billows You are tempest-tossed,
When you are discouraged, Thinking all is lost,
Count your many blessings, Name them one by one,
And it will surprise you What the Lord has done.

[Refrain]
Count your blessings, Name them one by one,
Count your blessings, See what God has done!
Count your blessings, Name them one by one,
*And it will surprise you what the Lord hath done.**

---

* "Count Your Blessings," words by Johnson Oatman Jr., public domain (in Songs for Young People, by Edwin Excell [Chicago, Illinois: Curts & Jennings, 1897], number 34), http://www.hymntime.com.

CHAPTER 13

Family Physical Recovery

For I am sure that neither death nor life,
nor angels nor rulers,
nor things present nor things to come,
nor powers, nor height nor depth,
nor anything else in all creation,
will be able to separate us
from the love of God in Christ Jesus our Lord.
—ROMANS 8:38–39

Any incident like the magnitude of our wreck causes numerous changes on multiple levels for each person involved. I've mentioned spiritual blessings, so here's a brief word about the physical recovery of all four of us. Monty was not the only one injured in our family, though his injuries were by far the most severe. At

the time of the wreck, our sons were reclining on
their foam bed in the back of our station wagon.
Each had his head on a pillow. Thus they were very
protected during the impact.

Charles, our seven-year-old, complained that
he was not injured enough to get all the fuss and
attention like everyone else. He wanted to use the
wheelchair and have X-rays taken. Mostly he was
very shaken up.

David, our six-year-old, had his head and an ear
banged on the side of the car. This gave us concern,
but nothing physical showed up at the first hospital.
Concerned, we watched him closely and later
became aware that our joyful little songbird could no
longer carry a tune. After many tests and discussions
with doctors, we were told there wasn't any physical
damage. Yet the trauma of the whole situation had
somehow affected his ability to match musical tones.
A specialist told us that over the years he would
most likely gradually regain his singing ability. Sure
enough, now in his fifties, David sings along with
the congregation of his church with great gusto.

Before the wreck Monty was in great physical
shape because the Texas college had a racquetball court
he took advantage of many days each week. Several

of the mathematics faculty were fiercely competitive on the racquetball court, and he flourished in that physical competition. Thus, both his upper body and lower body strength were extremely good. He had also frequented the weight room with the students and other faculty during the months prior to the wreck.

We couldn't have picked a better time during the school schedule for Monty to be out of commission for so long. As a college teacher, he only had a few classes to teach before Christmas because the fall semester was winding down, and students were preparing for their final exams. While Monty was still in the hospital, his colleagues were able to cover his few remaining classes. He was able to create his own final exams, grade them, and figure out the final grades for all his students.

Since we arrived home before Christmas, he had several weeks before the spring semester started. By the beginning of the second semester in January, he progressed enough to return to the classroom. Monty could be a very animated teacher. So I worried about his balancing on one foot while writing mathematical proofs on the blackboard with chalk in his right hand and a crutch in his left. Since I'm qualified,

I volunteered to teach his classes for him until he recovered more. However, he was determined to do it himself. He succeeded—with no falls that I know about.

Midway through the spring semester he got the doctor's permission to begin going without the crutches as he was able to tolerate the pain in the injured leg. He did so immediately. To my horror, he walked out of the doctor's office holding both crutches high in the air to prove that he could do it.

The Paris doctors had coordinated with those in Houston for Monty to continue his physical therapy with a local doctor through the spring and summer. Monty was so determined to regain full use of his left leg that he diligently did all the physical therapy—plus even more. I often walked into the living room and found him sitting in a chair with his hands locked below his left knee—pulling on his lower leg so that it bent farther than it wanted to go. Tears would be trickling down his face because of the pain. Even if it was self-inflicted pain, I couldn't stand to watch. I had to leave the room. And he would call out through clenched teeth, "No pain, no gain!"

Apparently, he was correct because he regained the full use of the leg and knee. Within two years, he was doing about anything he wanted to do, including all the hiking we did as a family, like backpacking down into the Grand Canyon during Christmas break three years later. Since he was the assistant leader for our sons' Boy Scout troop, his activities included several 125-mile bike hikes and a week of hiking at Philmont Scout Ranch in addition to numerous canoeing and rock-climbing trips with the scouts. He didn't allow *anything* to slow him down.

Charles (16) and David (15)
after both attained Eagle Scout in 1984

Author's husband, Monty,
at Philmont Scout Ranch

I, on the other hand, had different types of injuries
that lasted for years. I had been briefly knocked
unconscious in the collision but had no broken
bones. Mainly, I had nerve damage to the left arm and
shoulder that left me with recurring pain for years and
now returns whenever I'm too close to EMF (electric
and magnetic fields) for very long. At the time of the
crash, I was bent down with my head on a level with
the padded part of the dashboard. Somehow, the top

of my head received a rug-type burn to the scalp that caused hair problems for quite some time. But it also gave rise to my feeling really loved by God.

Let me explain. A few days before we left on the fateful Thanksgiving trip, I went into one of our large department stores to finish my Christmas shopping. On my way through the store, I noticed a wig on display with a special sale sign. I chuckled to myself. The wig was precisely my hair color and styled exactly how I wore my hair. On the way out of the store, I again passed the wig counter and noticed that the sale price was extremely low. I felt prompted to buy it but dismissed the idea and took my packages to the car. Why would I wear a wig?

However, I still had a strong feeling I should buy the wig, even though I didn't need—or want—one. I returned to the store twice to look and even examine the wig as I fought with myself on how silly it was for me to buy a wig. Finally, deciding perhaps the Lord had a reason for me to buy the wig, I returned to the store and purchased it.

A few days later, the car wreck gave the top of my head a burn, like a carpet burn, that broke and burned the hair off the top of my head. In 1975 no woman wanted to go around, even temporarily, with the top of her head having no hair or with the short stubble as it slowly grew back. But guess what? I had a wig so close to my hair color and style that no one was aware I had lost part of my hair. I simply put on the wig when I made the quick trip home to get the boys back in school.

This probably sounds silly—especially to a man. However, as a female, I felt intimately loved and cherished by God because of this provision.

Scripture talks about how God knows the hairs on your head. Now I realized he even knows the color of my hair and the style I wear it.

He knew I would need a wig and in planning ahead, He provided not only the right color, but also the correct style. Not only does God love me, but He respectfully knows me—an insignificant mortal.

This was one more example clearly illustrating to me that God was looking after our many personal needs. This deep truth has slowly percolated into the deep recesses of my being. I'm wrapped securely in God's love whether I feel it or not. My emotions have nothing to do with it. God is always with me.

Since our parents and the home we were raised in affect our view of God and especially our view of His love, I was blessed as a child to have a father who always made me feel loved and protected. Then in my mid-twenties I met and married Monty, who did much to give me a sense of being loved and protected. Now I was slowly awakening to the fact that God loves and protects me in ways mere humans can't. I treasure this realization deep in my soul.

The mighty Lord of angel armies is on my side! I am loved!

> *The love of God is greater far*
> *Than tongue or pen could ever tell;*
> *It goes beyond the highest star,*
> *and reaches to the lowest hell;*
> *The guilty pair, bowed down with care,*
> *God gave His Son to win;*
> *His erring child He reconciled,*
> *and pardoned from his sin.*

> [Refrain]
> *Oh, love of God, how rich and pure!*
> *How measureless and strong!*
> *It shall forevermore endure*
> *The saints' and angels' song.*

---

* "The Love of God," words by Frederick M. Lehman, public domain, 1917 (in Songs That Are Different, Volume 2, 1919), http://www.hymntime.com.

CHAPTER 14

God's Hand in Christmas

Whoever has the Son has life;
whoever does not have the Son of God
does not have life.
I write these things to you who believe
in the name of the Son of God,
that you may know that you have eternal life.
−1 JOHN 5:12−13

After the wreck our family was finally together under one roof, just in time for Christmas.

Lord, please help me make everything feel as normal as possible for the boys. I don't know how this may be affecting them. They've had so many changes. Leaving all their close friends in a small town to move to a suburb of Houston. Riding a bus after they used to walk to school and everywhere safely. Living for weeks with the family of new friends. How do I make Christmas feel normal?

Following my usual practice, I had finished the family Christmas shopping before Thanksgiving, so everyone had a gift under our hastily erected tree. Since a Christmas tree had been important in our homes when Monty and I were growing up, we continued the tradition. However, we attempted to do things to emphasize Christ and the celebration of His birth. Therefore, our decorating and festivities were as Christ-centered as possible. This emphasis meant that while the boys were young, we had a birthday cake at an empty seat at the table and sang "Happy Birthday" to Jesus. The boys and I baked and fixed treats for friends and neighbors. And as we were able, we sang carols and went to special Christmas worship services.

When the boys were toddlers, I had designed a wall-hanging Advent calendar with pockets for tiny ornaments, many of which I made. Each day they hung another miniature ornament on the green, tree-shaped part of the cloth calendar. I used the various ornaments to help me explain different things related to the Christmas season and the birth of Christ.

*David and Charles putting ornaments on
Advent Calendar the author made*

Among our Christmas decorations, I always used
varying sizes and styles of creches all over the house,
at least one in each room. We used them to remind
all of us that Jesus Christ had indeed come in the
flesh. As the days progressed, we further used them
to remind us to discuss His deity, His virgin birth,
and why He was born. We tried to mention some

of the many different prophesies fulfilled in the life of the one man Jesus—and especially that some of the prophecies were 700 years before his miraculous birth. Monty and I believed it was important to remind each of us regarding just how faithful God had been to His promises. This baby of Bethlehem revealed the heart of God the Father to us. Although people often didn't see or understand the significance of a particular time, later history showed us that the God who sees from the beginning to the end had a plan that had precision and order, as well as purpose.

Near the tree, we always had our small Nativity set with plastic characters that the children were free to play with, and they and visitors often did. In later years, we had a particular manger scene in the living room where we gathered our gifts. It was where Monty would read Scripture and give a short devotional. Years later we added Advent candles and the new tradition of the shepherd's pouch. On Christmas Eve we would all put our gifts to Christ in small bags (shepherds' pouches) beside the manger in the same manner we imagined the shepherds brought gifts to the Messiah. Then we used the shepherds' pouch gifts to help someone outside the family or a charity. On Christmas morning, the boys received a small gift in their bag to symbolize the gifts God showers on us.

Yet something about the Christmas after the wreck was significantly different for me, as much as I tried to make it normal. Perhaps it was my motherly instinct after a close call with death. It wasn't enough for me to just see everyone with my eyes. I needed to touch them physically. The boys probably got tired of my repeatedly stroking or hugging them to make sure this wasn't a dream. We really were home . . . and all together again.

On a deeply personal level, I understood the tinsel and gifts didn't make Christmas exceptional, nor did our special meal or unique church service and caroling. Somehow, for me, it was coming together as a family and celebrating in remembrance what our Savior did out of His totally pure, unconditional love for us. I tried so hard to recapture normal Christmas, but there still seemed to be something missing for me. What was it? I couldn't put my finger on it.

A few days after Christmas, Monty was resting while the boys played outside, and the house was quiet. I was picking up around the house when I noticed a ray of sunlight coming through the front picture window. It caused a small tree ornament on the floor to sparkle. As I stepped into that ray of light to pick up the ornament, the sun streaming through the window reflected off the shiny metal. I paused and studied it with its small metal cut-out shapes of Mary, Joseph, and baby. It nestled in my hand as I savored the warm Texas sun spilling through the window. Basking in that warmth, I thought of all the ways God had gone before us, day after day, and all the ways He had repeatedly shown me His love and provision.

I felt as I imagined a seed might feel in the sun's warming light when all the potential genetic information stored inside it begins to direct it upward and skyward in response to the sunlight. Its tender shoots and leaves dance in the warmth of the sunlight, calling them to bud and bloom in the warm and welcoming rays. I was not only soaking in sunlight, but also S-o-n-light.

The individual facts from my years of reading Scripture and hearing it taught were swirling together into one powerful truth surging through me. This bud was swelling and bursting forth into a deeper comprehension that was giving me exuberant joy.

I fondled the ornament and thought about how the same God who had created the sun warming my skin, loved me so much that He provided a way to restore fellowship with Him. And the baby on this ornament represented His Son, Jesus Christ. This long-awaited   God-wrapped-in-human-form-baby was the Messiah promised thousands of years before he arrived in Bethlehem. He physically came to earth to show God's great love. He died for us to return us to fellowship with God. He rose from the dead—and now lives forever.

I placed the small nativity ornament back on the tree as my spirit soared to new heights.

I serve a risen Savior who's truly alive and loves me! He really . . . actually . . . loves me!

Hope and joy flooded my soul! Whatever had caused my unsettled feeling earlier was now gone. In His infinite wisdom, God knew I needed this extra affirmation. Somehow, during that moment in the sunlight, Christmas, Good Friday, and Easter merged into one glorious understanding. Perhaps it all had something to do with coming face to face with the fragility of human life and staring death in the face. But now I knew beyond the shadow of a doubt my joy, hope, and confidence were in relying on the one true God. And He had already demonstrated that He can raise the dead. My hope was, and is, in a risen Savior who has repeatedly shown me tangibly that He *is* with me, and not only is He *not* silent, He also knows me and loves me and promises His followers eternal life.

During the weeks following the wreck, when God showed me love in ways I had never thought about before, His love flowed from an immense compassion that a human simply can never match. Now I realized that God was there even when I felt alone. He never deserted me, even when my circumstances were scary and painful. I personally learned the same lesson Peter learned when Jesus asked him to step out of the boat and walk on the water: You must keep your eyes on the Lord and *not* your physical circumstances if you're going to survive and thrive.

Since the wreck, Christmas has continued to be a special time of getting together as a family. Some of the best times of life are shared around the table with loved ones. Yes, we may have points of disagreement, but God enables love to work through all of them. After the boys married and grandchildren came along, we scattered across the country but still managed to get together every other Christmas.

Author, Phyllis Kester, and her husband, Monty,
shortly before their fiftieth wedding anniversary

Years later in 2013, as I started making plans
for the approaching fiftieth wedding anniversary
Monty and I would have in March of 2014, I began
feeling I shouldn't plan a family get-together on our
anniversary. I repeatedly sensed that someone in our
immediate family circle would be gone, probably
before our fiftieth anniversary. As I tried to reason
it out logically, it seemed most logical to me that it
might be one of us older ones or one of our three
teenage grandsons since boys tend to have risky
behavior.

Suspecting the 2013 family Christmas might be the last time all three generations would be together at our house, I hired a photographer. I emphasized that I wanted her to take a large number of group photos and photos of every one of the family members.

Charles, Monty, and David Kester,
Christmas 2013

Something else important happened at that family Christmas of 2013. Shortly after Monty and I had married nearly fifty years earlier, he had given me a leather Thompson Chain-Reference Study Bible. My heavy use of it for almost five decades had rendered it into a loose-leaf Bible. My elder son, Charles, although a successful lawyer, had the hobby of restoring and selling valuable old religious books.

"Charles, do you think you could restore my Bible?"

He scrutinized it. "Sure, Mom. I think so."

Although he was a very responsible adult, somewhere in the depths of my mothering heart, he would always be a child. So it was with reluctance that I let him take it. He was about to carry my precious study Bible out of my house and halfway across the country. Would I ever see it again?

About two months later he was cleaning snow off his driveway and had a nasty fall on the ice. Before an ambulance managed to maneuver the long and treacherous icy roads to get to him and then take him to the hospital, a blood clot formed and blocked his lungs. Our healthy forty-six-year-old Charles suddenly and unexpectedly died.

Nothing describes the unspeakable shock and pain of a parent losing a child. Yet I thanked God for the profusion of pictures and the many love-filled memories we had as a family. Of inexpressible comfort was the precious gift that Charles gave me. When Monty and I flew to Arkansas to be with his wife,

Cheryl, after Charles died, she presented my restored Bible as a gift from Charles. The weekend he died was the same weekend he finished restoring my Bible for me. Now this gift is even more special. It was initially from my husband, was restored by my son, and holds half a century of personal marginal notes regarding God's faithfulness to me in answered prayers.

Charles Kester's Columbarium marker

As I had strangely sensed, Christmas 2013 was indeed the last time all our three generations would gather together on earth, but I look forward to an eventual reunion in heaven. I drew, and I still draw, great comfort from the assurance I will see Charles again in the future.

> *My hope is built on nothing less*
> *Than Jesus' blood and righteousness.*
> *I dare not trust the sweetest frame,*
> *But wholly trust in Jesus' name.*

> *When darkness seems to hide His face,*
> *I rest on His unchanging grace.*
> *In every high and stormy gale,*
> *My anchor holds within the veil.*

> *When He shall come with trumpet sound,*
> *Oh may I then in Him be found.*
> *Dressed in His righteousness alone,*
> *Faultless to stand before the throne.*

> [Refrain]
> *On Christ the solid rock I stand,*
> *All other ground is sinking sand;*
> *All other ground is sinking sand.*

---

* "My Hope Is Built," words by Edward Mote, public domain, circa 1834 (first published in Mote's Hymns of Praise, 1836), http://www.hymntime. com.

CHAPTER 15

Lessons Learned

One generation shall commend your works to another,
and shall declare your mighty deeds.
—PSALM 145:4

Part 1: Pivotal Decisions

The previous pages have recounted incidents in the lives of an ordinary American family in their journey with an extraordinary God. During the course of our everyday lives, Monty and I lived through a series of occurrences that proved to be a truly defining experience because as our faith was challenged, it grew like a muscle being exercised.

From my present perspective of over eight decades, life is not one large mountain to conquer; it is a range of mountains with valleys—sometimes deep valleys—in between. In hindsight, I now see how each mountain and valley strengthened and equipped me for the next one because the God of the mountains was still there with me through the valleys.

Just as we had to learn the alphabet before we could build words and sentences on the foundation of knowing our letters, our walk with the Lord also builds on foundational concepts and decisions. At any point in time, we're each the sum of choices and responses we've made. Some of those earlier decisions were pivotal in my journey of life. Over time those seemingly small decisions compound like financial investments and determine where we end up.

In my mind there appear to be four pivotal decision points that happened early in my pilgrimage before the wreck, and they laid the foundation for what I learned through the time of the wreck.

Pivotal Decision Point 1:

The foundation upon which everything was built was my understanding of the importance of God's Word, the Bible.

I accepted the fact that "All Scripture is breathed out by God and profitable for teaching, for reproof, for correction, and for training in righteousness, that the man of God may be complete, equipped for every good work" (2 Timothy 3:16–17). Furthermore, I recognized that God's Word really was a lamp to my feet and a light to my path (Psalm 119:105).

On many occasions Monty and I discussed how God reveals Himself through the Bible, through creation, and through life's circumstances. Monty once summed up our view of Scripture quite well from a mathematical point of view when he typed up what he called the ground of hope for life. He began with, "I accept the Scripture as a mathematician accepts the axioms for the system he is going to work in."

Pivotal Decision Point 2:

Believing Jesus to be my Savior.

God, because of His deep affection for us, made it simple to become a Christ-follower, or Christian. All I had to do was believe in Jesus as my Savior—not just intellectually believe, but with commitment. That meant I accepted His death as the sufficient sacrifice for my sins (John 3:16) and fully trusted Him alone as my Savior (John 14:6; Acts 4:11–12). In other words, I fully entrusted my spiritual wellbeing to Jesus Christ and believed in my heart that God had raised Him from the dead (Romans 10:9). It is this personal relationship with Jesus Christ through faith that made me a Christian.

Pivotal Decision Point 3:

Choosing to let God be in total control rather than my obeying only what I want to obey.

This step of faith means becoming submissive to Jesus and allowing Him and scriptural truth to permeate all aspects of my daily life. This decision of my obedience was made in advance rather than waiting to see if I liked what God was going to ask of me.

Over the years I've learned to pray with the attitude that I want what Jesus wants, for He knows what's best for me and for His purposes. I've also had to learn that His answer and His direction come in His timing, not mine. I'm repeatedly reminded that God often opens the door I want to go through just before my nose bumps into it—never way in advance as I would like, the way things happened each time we needed an ambulance.

Pivotal Decision Point 4:

Recognizing and removing the idols or whatever competes for the primary place in my heart instead of God.

It was humbling when I recognized that I was not putting God first in everything. In my case I had to recognize and demonstrate to God that I would relinquish my tight hold on those I loved. It was a test to demonstrate what I actually believed and that my heart was fully after the Lord.

Part 2: Six Lessons Taught through This Experience

Lesson 1:

Be Bold and Confident

*I am not ashamed, because I know in
whom I have put my trust,
and I have no doubt at all that he is able to safeguard
until that Day what I have entrusted to him.*
−2 TIMOTHY 1:12 NJB

*[Jesus said] do not fear those who kill the body
but cannot kill the soul.
Rather fear him who can destroy
both soul and body in hell.*
−MATTHEW 10:28

As believers, Monty and I knew life
and death are in the hands of our sovereign
Lord. However, our miraculous survival made

us aware on a deeper level of what it means when someone says, "Nothing will remove you from this life as long as God is not finished with you." It does not mean you will not suffer or go through tough times, for Scripture indicates suffering is an inevitable part of life, even the Christian life. What altered was our perspective regarding fear of circumstances or people. We both came away with a new boldness and confidence in the Lord, for He had protected us and must still have a purpose for our lives.

This fearless confidence gave us the strength and faith we needed to trust God for the things He had planned for us—especially during the thirteen years we lived in the Houston area. Many things came our way that we never sought or expected to do. For example, Monty found he could schedule some of his college teaching load to be math classes taught to male prisoners inside the Ellis prison unit in the Texas Department of Criminal Justice prison north of Huntsville, Texas. His college was giving Texas inmates the opportunity of getting a college education while behind bars since it had been shown to reduce their return to prison after release. When teaching inside the prison walls, Monty would close his classroom door and not let the guards and their guns inside his actual classroom because he wanted his students' experience to be as much like a real college classroom as he could make it—even though at least a couple of his students were in for murder. As you can imagine, I did a lot a praying whenever Monty went to Huntsville to teach in the prison, but some rewarding and interesting experiences came out of those years.

This new boldness was a very profound change for me because I had tended to be a shy introvert and would never have imagined being tapped to be on the Greater Houston Advisory Board for Campus Crusade and several local district educational advisory committees. I also worked with Vonette Bright, wife of Bill Bright, and Beverly LaHaye chose me as one of several speakers at the second Concerned Women for America annual conference in Washington, DC.

The Lord knew Monty and I would both need bold confidence to do His will. He used the time period around the wreck to strengthen our faith and give both of us the confident boldness to do whatever He asked, for now we recognized we were part of something much bigger than ourselves.

Lesson 2:

Kick Fearfulness out the Door

For God has not given us a spirit of fear,
but of power and of love and of a sound mind.
−2 TIMOTHY 1:7 NKJV

There is no fear in love, but perfect love casts out fear.
For fear has to do with punishment,
and whoever fears has not been perfected in love.
−1 JOHN 4:18

This new confident boldness helped me begin acting on the knowledge that fear is not from God. Unbridled fear can be a large obstacle, whether fear of the unknown, fear of being alone, or fear of others' opinions. It can be a brutal taskmaster because it can cripple and enslave if you allow it to take over your thinking.

I found that as my trust and affection for God grew, so did my concept of how big God is. Consequently, fear shrank into the background. Wouldn't I be safest in the arms of the One who cares most for me? This realization freed me from the bondage of the fear of death for myself or others because I learned God goes with me through whatever happens. On "the other side," I'll be with the Lord Jesus Christ and the believing loved ones who've preceded me.

Lesson 3:

Realize That Problem and Solution Come Together

> *None of the trials which have come upon you*
> *is more than a human being can stand.*
> *You can trust that God will not let you*
> *be put to the test beyond your strength,*
> *but* with *any trial will also provide a way*
> *out by enabling you to put up with it.*
> −1 CORINTHIANS 10:13 NJB
> [EMPHASIS ADDED]

First Corinthians 10:13 brought an important new understanding for me when I kept finding solutions already provided for my needs as I've described them—sometimes even before I became aware I had a need. This verse points out that I won't have any problem or trial beyond my ability to stand it, but more important is the word *with* in that passage. It points out that from God's perspective, my problem and my way out come hand-in-hand *with* each other.

The experience of the wreck increased my understanding of how—when I the believer face tests and problems—God used this teachable situation to help me grow. After all, He has my undivided attention during difficult times. Simply being a believer does not protect me from disasters, plagues, floods, earthquakes, or heartache. But these are events where I can practice faithfulness to God and experience His sustaining me through the experience.

From God's perspective, He has already provided the solution to my upcoming problem, and I will discover that solution once I learn whatever I'm supposed to learn through the situation. I've found that if I ask God to help me see the difficulty through His eyes, I may even notice the quality things He is trying to teach me through the predicament. If I'm a quick learner, the situation seems to resolve faster.

Lesson 4:

Treasure Love, Death, and Hope

> But you, O LORD,
> are a God merciful and gracious,
> slow to anger and abounding
> in steadfast love and faithfulness.
> —PSALM 86:15

> Blessed be the God and Father
> of our Lord Jesus Christ!
> According to his great mercy, he has caused us
> to be born again to a living hope through
> the resurrection of Jesus Christ from the dead,
> to an inheritance that is imperishable,
> undefiled, and unfading, kept in heaven for you,
> who by God's power are being guarded through faith
> for a salvation ready to be revealed in the last time.
> —1 PETER 1:3–5

One thing I experienced over and over was realizing, with gratitude, that God was always doing more than seen at the moment. Various circumstances repeatedly displayed God's power and loving intentions toward us. Not only was, and is, God real and trustworthy, but I also recognized a pattern of kind provision whenever Monty, the boys, or I had a need.

I began learning to recognize His hand directing behind the scenes. He was always present and active in every circumstance regardless of how I felt, and He was actively bringing forth what eventually showed up to be the best for me. His revelation of who He is and seeing His abundant mercy and sovereignty became priceless gifts.

For example, intellectually I knew we all eventually die, but the death of Jesus was different. He claimed to be God and promised to return to life after three days as proof of who He said He was. Following His death by crucifixion, His distraught disciples saw Him walking around alive a few days later. They became transformed into bold proclaimers of His resurrection. The actual historical evidence of His resurrection is so strong that many who have attempted to disprove it eventually became convinced of its historical validity. And it was His resurrection that gave me a reason, and confident expectation, for hope. It showed me He had power over death. In Jesus Christ I found the fulfillment of the scriptural promises, and in His resurrection I found the living hope that is energizing, alive and active in the soul of the believer.

On a whole different level I began to see that the expression of His deep affection through His life, death, and resurrection is only the beginning of His demonstration of compassion for His children. I was catching a glimpse of how God truly loves me personally, and it's not just words written on paper. I became aware that my life depends upon the Lord Jesus Christ more than it depends upon breath. During these difficult times, I came to treasure Jesus for only the resurrected Jesus can take the fractured painful pieces of our lives and fill them with the healing story of hope and redemption.

Author, Phyllis, with her parents:
Buel and Hallie Smith

Since I grew up as an only child, the whole concept of family has always been important to me, but the wreck somehow affected even my concept of family. There seemed to be a different dimension to my feeling of family. I still believe that sound families are a key ingredient to the stability of society and that a family, just like a marriage, requires work. But something deep within me changed forever once I truly understood—not just intellectually, but within every fiber of my being—that at any second one of my family could be dead. Yet I no longer had anxiety or fear. I was at peace about my own future and that of my immediate family members. There was such peace and hope in knowing that each of them personally knew Jesus as their Savior. I find it encouraging to know that I will see them again in eternity because they believe in Jesus and His resurrection. This hope beyond the grave is a powerful present hope permeating my whole being. It takes away any fear or anxiety about death and the unknown. I have confidence I will see them again even after death.

Three generations walk on the beach

There is another way the wreck affected my attitude toward family and friends. I began understanding how urgent it is to cherish one another in each moment while we still have the opportunity here on the physical earth. Disagreeing with someone doesn't make us enemies. Instead, we need to work on the skill of disagreeing agreeably and not letting misunderstandings or hurt feelings go unaddressed. We can have unity without uniformity. We should resolve differences quickly because relationships are so precious—relationships with each other as well as with Christ.

Lesson 5:

Understand How to View Bad Things

In Luke 13:1–5 Jesus was asked about two bad situations in which people were killed—by Pilate and when a tower fell on them. The questioners wanted to know the meaning of these tragedies and deaths. Jesus' answer was shocking because He turned the tables and indicated the meaning of these disasters related to those living and asking the questions. In both cases, He answered their questions with, "Unless you repent, you will all likewise perish." His answer indicated that the meaning of the disasters was for everyone still living for twice he repeated the message, "Repent [of your own sinfulness] or perish." He seemed to indicate

that those disasters were a gracious summons from God
to repent and be saved while there was still time.

In Houston, somewhere around the time of our wreck, the elderly Corrie ten Boom spoke to a small group of us ladies. She was a Dutch concentration camp survivor who had protected Jews from the Nazis during World War II by hiding them in her home. Later she became a renowned Christian leader, known for her teachings on forgiveness and the story of her survival, *The Hiding Place*. Corrie held up a beautiful woven tapestry that we all admired. Then she turned it around to reveal the ugly tangled threads on the back. She pointed out how each of our lives is like one of those colored threads in the tapestry as it intersects with other threads—people's lives. Since we're all on the finite, earthly side of the tapestry, we only see the tangled mess of threads and knots, but God is looking on the other, eternal, side and sees the beautiful pattern He is weaving with all our lives.

The tapestry image has helped me keep things in perspective. Now I try to look at my difficult times as one of those "knots" in the thread of the beautiful tapestry God is weaving. I remind myself that God will never waste a knot or difficulty without accomplishing all the good He desires.

Lesson 6:

Remember Jesus is the center of life and cannot be destroyed

At that time his voice shook the earth,
but now he has promised, "Yet once more
I will shake not only the earth but also the heavens."
This phrase, "Yet once more," indicates
the removal of things that are shaken—that is,
things that have been made—in order that the things
that cannot be shaken may remain.
−HEBREWS 12:26–27

For it stands in Scripture:
"Behold, I am laying in Zion a stone,
a cornerstone chosen and precious,
and whoever believes in him
will not be put to shame."
−1 PETER 2:6

*"This Jesus is the stone that was rejected by you,
the builders, which has become the cornerstone.
And there is salvation in no one else, for there is
no other name under heaven given among men
by which we must be saved."*
−ACTS 4:11−12

It was after the wreck that I matured in my faith enough to realize that if I follow the Lord closely, He actually prepares me ahead of time for whatever is coming and is with me as I go through it.

In a time of intense difficulty, the pain of a crisis sometimes shakes us to our core. It may even cause cracks or destroy whatever is at the center of our being. Picture a wagon wheel. I could remove some of the spokes of that wheel, yet it still functions because it still has the center hub. The *center* of the wheel is critical for its proper functioning. Likewise, whatever is at the center of my life is just as critical for my functioning. A center of temporary things, like people, philosophy, or possessions, would let me down. But the permanence of God as the true center of my life will withstand the crises. I don't want to put my confidence in that which can be destroyed.

That was why God was impressing me before the wreck that my center needed to be corrected. It had to be only God, not God plus something else. It's like Matthew 7:24–27 in Scripture. Jesus was explaining that everyone who heard or read His words (Scripture) and was obedient to His teaching was like the wise man who built his house on the rock so that no storms could destroy it. Whatever is at our center forms the foundation upon which we base our life. We need a solid rock foundation or center that cannot be shaken. I shudder to think of how ill-equipped I would have been for the wreck if I hadn't relinquished my heart and will to God ahead of time.

If you've ever wondered, "Where is God?" during your time of crisis, I hope reading this will encourage you to trace His hand as you travel on your journey. I've seen God's invisible hand at work numerous times over my eight decades, and I adore catching a glimpse of the fact that we are children of an amazing and loving God. I have found He really does go before us and is present with His children.

As we face tragedies that come our way, let us open our eyes to what God may be trying to reveal to us. We need to be sober-minded as we ask Him to help us discern what His purposes are in all that happens. We want Him to accomplish all the good He desires as we deal with the present difficulty or messy-looking knots on the backside of His tapestry. If we stay close and keep our eyes on Him, He continually reveals His heart and His hand.

Author & husband enjoying the outdoors

Blessed assurance, Jesus is mine!
O what a foretaste of glory divine!
Heir of salvation, purchase of God,
Born of His Spirit, washed in His blood.

Perfect submission, perfect delight,
Visions of rapture now burst on my sight;
Angels descending, bring from above
Echoes of mercy, whispers of love.

Perfect submission, all is at rest,
I in my Savior am happy and blest,
Watching and waiting, looking above,
Filled with His goodness, lost in His love.

[Refrain]
This is my story, this is my song,
Praising my Savior all the day long;
This is my story, this is my song,
*Praising my Savior all the day long.**

---

* "Blessed Assurance," words by Fanny J. Crosby, public domain, 1873, http://www.hymntime.com.

Legacy of the Wreck Update

*May the God of hope fill you
with all joy and peace in believing,
so that by the power of the Holy Spirit
you may abound in hope.*
−ROMANS 15:13

During the 2020–21 Covid shutdown, my husband and I used the time to reminisce over our fifty-seven years of marriage with all its joys, twists, and turns. It was perfect timing for me to write *Tracing God's Hand* because tracing God's hand in our lives was exactly what we were doing during much of our confined time.

Then came another sudden event.

On Sunday, April 25, 2021, while still in a semi-lockdown, I was dressed and watching the early morning streaming of our church service. Pastor Nathan Smith was preaching from Hebrews 4 about entering into God's rest, which will eventually be heaven. I was delighted with the sermon, but puzzled that Monty was still in the hot tub instead of watching the service with me. Afterward, I shut off the computer and went to find out why he was still in the hot tub. I found him non-responsive. He had actually entered his eternal rest with the Lord while I was merely hearing about how wonderful it would be.

Words cannot describe the shock and brokenhearted heartache of suddenly realizing my loving mate of fifty-seven years was no longer with me. I have no words to adequately describe the big hole it leaves in my heart. It feels like an amputation that has ripped off at least half of me—the better half. Although I knew Monty looked forward to going to be with the Lord, and there would prove to be lots of friends and family to support me after his death, how do you face the future stretching out before you without your soulmate? Or the birthdays, anniversaries, and holidays with all the special things

we did? I'll never smell his Old Spice aftershave
when he pulls me close. How do I face that lonely
bed where we've slept nestled like spoons for years?
Grief carries an intense feeling of aloneness.

It's by God's grace and being wrapped in the
prayers of loving friends and family that I made it
through the first months. One sweet friend bought
me one of those long body-length pillows so there
would be something else in that big, lonely bed
besides me—yes, it helped, but it didn't smell like
Old Spice.

I can't imagine trying to go through such loss
without a close relationship with God, for if there
is one lesson very clear to my mind after tracing
God's provision through the years, it is to cast all
my cares on God, for He truly does love and care for
me (1 Peter 5:7). I've come to realize He really never
leaves me or forsakes me—no matter what.

But how do we deal with such loss? All our
lives we've dealt with growth coupled with loss and
turning things loose. Often as we reach out for
something new, we must turn loose something old:
we move to new locations, we marry, children grow
up and leave home. But as we age, it becomes more
turning loose without the growth. At that point we're

dealing with the loss of mobility, hearing, memory, or loved ones. During the pandemic we saw so much grief engulfing families. Ever new types of loss have occurred, often coupled with fear and isolation.

Regardless of our type of loss, we don't walk alone even though we may feel isolated. God is with us and has given us great men and women of faith to encourage us. It may be family members, friends, a church leader, or it may be some of the people of faith in Scripture or in Christian books. It's good to reach out to them when we are in spiritual need, as well as taking our need to God.

As I wrestled with the different types of loss, it forced me to rethink what is truly important to me when the whole world seems to be in a state of crisis. I concluded that it is central to my life to have meaning and hope, and I choose to look to the Creator of the universe to give me both.

In my own loss I am grateful that Monty was a child of God. This means I have the *hope*—through Christ and His resurrection—that I will see him again someday in eternity with Christ.

As for *meaning*, I look to God, Scripture, and the created world around me. I've found great comfort in Scripture. Through it, God reminds me that in nature there is an instructive picture. The metamorphosis of a butterfly is very applicable for instruction whenever we go through a big change.

I've come to identify with the butterfly slowly emerging from its cocoon in which everything it previously knew as a crawling creature has to be re-purposed into what it needs in its new form of a flying creature. All the old ways of doing things, like crawling, are replaced by a new normal, wings for flying. I think the melt-down and re-organization during the time in the cocoon is a good picture of what's happening during the grieving process. For the butterfly, there are new roles, new adventures, and new horizons to be explored. I've accepted Monty's death and my grief as part of the normal process of life—the melting down and re-forming. Now I'm trying to look at life through butterfly eyes. God still has a purpose for me, or He wouldn't have left me here. So it's time for me to flap my butterfly wings courageously and look for new horizons to be explored. I do not despair in small beginnings for the joy of the Lord is my strength. I've learned that circumstances do not dictate my joy, and I'm not done becoming.

***

Now, how does all this relate to the wreck?

As the days and weeks passed, I began seeing several patterns related to the wreck.

1. First, a video slide show of about seventy pictures that our eldest grandson and Charles' widow put together for Monty's funeral showed pictures of him as hymns played in the background. This is sometimes done at funerals to give people a view of the individual's entire life. Monty's slide show was left on the Tharp Funeral Home website for weeks, and I found myself repeatedly going back, day after day, to watch the ten-minute video. I would watch with tears trickling down my face, but—to my amazement— there was such peace and joy in repeatedly watching. "Why is this?" I kept asking myself.

Included among the pictures was our wrecked vehicle from 1975. That photo triggered my memory of all God taught both of us through that time in our lives. I knew Monty had become a Christian about the time we married in our mid-twenties. Watching those snapshots from his life caused a thought to crystallize in my mind.

It was as if I looked through a pair of binoculars that changed what I saw. My natural eyes see only from a natural perspective, and I may even think I am seeing everything. However, when I put binoculars to my eyes, there is so much more to see. God, through His Holy Spirit within believers, gives us the ability to see things through spiritual eyes—much as when we look through binoculars and see things we didn't perceive at first.

Watching the video visually reminded me that we are each an uncut diamond at the beginning of our life. God sees the hidden, potential jewel within each of us. Once we accept Christ as our Savior and trust our lives to Him for His direction, He goes *with* us through various situations that knock off some of the sharp edges and shape us. That wreck definitely shaped Monty in a number of ways. God then used people and circumstances like sandpaper for polishing away rough spots. Over our lifetime He uses all these challenging and painful situations to shape us into a glorious diamond that reflects our Creator's glory to others.

Watching pictures from Monty's life was like actually seeing him change from the diamond-in-the-rough to a jewel reflecting God to others. What joy to understand this grander view I was given access to. This has given me clarity and understanding. In difficult times, it is good to readjust our focus beyond what is raging around or within us. Bad things happen in our world, things over which we grieve, at times very deeply. However, those things do not shake my faith, and I hope you can say the same.

2. Second, I told how the Lord prepared me ahead of time for the wreck in chapter 2. In 1975 I recognized I must not hold onto my husband and children as the idols they had become, wanting God to protect them from any possible harm ever touching them. Now I understand how my action back *then* is greatly helping me *now*. Our past decisions truly do impact our future.

How is that possible? In 1975 I struggled with being obedient to God's Word and totally relinquishing my loved ones to His care. My heart had to be emptied of everything that mattered more to me than God. I was alone, wrestling, and God wanted my whole heart—not just part of it. I needed humility and needed to acknowledge my weakness. This transformed my relationship with God because that obedience became an entry point for His presence and power not only then, but later.

Scripture tells us in Romans 8:37 that through Christ, we are more than conquerors. That includes conquering fear of the unknown. Fear is not my master unless I allow it to be. Not only did that obedience prepare me for the wreck of 1975, it also sustained me in 2014 at my son's accidental death and again in 2021 at my husband's unexpected death.

One morning, shortly after Monty's death, I awoke with an exuberant joyful realization rolling over me and flooding my soul. I understood how the Lord had preserved my husband in 1975 for the additional forty-six years we had together before it was time for him finally to go home. I'm grateful for the extra time the Lord gave us together and am only—now—beginning to see the full legacy of that car wreck. It helped shape Monty into the God-reflecting jewel many described at his funeral, and it reinforced my strength of faith and hope for my own future. I realized God—in His timing—had spent forty-six years preparing me for this moment in time.

Many of us have experienced that special type of relationship with someone with whom our heart is so closely knit that words are not always needed to communicate—it can be a distinct look across the room, that raised eyebrow, or merely sensing their presence nearby. The same can be true in our relationship with God. I can certainly spend time in God's presence without saying a word out loud. Hearts don't always need words to communicate; they just need to be in unity. I want to know God in a personal way, not just know facts about Him. I hunger and thirst for the pleasure of His company in the deepest, most meaningful relationship I can find this side of heaven.

My own heart transformation came through intentional, individual decisions and quality quiet time spent alone with God, listening to Him, and learning of Him as I read and meditated on His Word. I'll never in my lifetime exhaust the depths of knowing Him. I want the Holy Spirit to show me how to pray as my grandmother did—not just weak prayers—but powerful prayers. May God's truth set us free from fear and uncertainty and enable us to view things not just through the lens of our emotions. Now I realize my happiness and peace depend upon Him—not on what I have or do or what others think or say (John 14:27). It seems that when I put away all my efforts to impress and simply come as a child to the Father that God responds quickly. When I draw near and choose to listen and obey, He draws near—even though I may not feel His presence sometimes.

3. *Third, what is the last legacy of the wreck for me? Music.* During the time since Monty's death, I have found music, especially the old hymns, to be an essential part of life. Sometimes I wake with a song or hymn wafting through my mind. This is probably because the latter stanzas of many of the older hymns express the foundation of hope that Scripture teaches: that Jesus Christ has gone ahead to prepare a place for us (John 14:1–3) and that one day we will join Him there (Matthew 25:34, Romans 10:13).

I described in chapter 6 how the music of praise and thanksgiving poured forth from my soul as I drove across Texas in 1975 while Monty waited for me in his hospital room. Today, I'm facing a similar private journey, although it's no longer merely along a Texas highway. Now I travel between the time of Christ's first coming and the time of His return, and I confidently say, "Although the love of my life awaits me in heaven instead of a hospital bed—I'm not alone, for the *Lover of my soul* is with me—*right now*—on this journey." I've come to realize that life is not all about living in ease, free of problems. Rather, it's about living according to God's Word in a unity of spirit with Him. May we each seriously consider, "Why do I believe what I believe, and does it line up with God's Word?"

I pray you'll join me on this pilgrimage toward heaven and God's free gift of eternal life through Jesus Christ our Lord (Romans 6:23b). May the music that filled my soul that night as I drove across Texas continue to strengthen and revive our spirits. May it fill us with God's love and peace regardless of our circumstances, for we have a loving Lord and Savior as our travel companion.

> *This is my Father's world,*
> *And to my listening ears*
> *All nature sings, and round me rings*
> *the music of the spheres.*
> *This is my Father's world:*
> *I rest me in the thought*
> *of rocks and trees, of skies and seas;*
> *His hand the wonders wrought.*
>
> *This is my Father's world:*
> *the birds their carols raise,*
> *the morning light, the lily white,*
> *Declare their Makers praise.*

This is my Father's world:
He shines in all that's fair;
In the rustling grass I hear Him pass,
He speaks to me everywhere.

This is my Father's world:
O let me ne'er forget
that though the wrong
Seems oft so strong,
God is the Ruler yet.
This is my Father's world:
The battle is not done:
Jesus who died shall be satisfied,
*And earth and Heav'n be one.**

---

*   "This Is My Father's World," words by Maltbie D. Babcock, public domain
    (Thoughts for Every-Day Living [New York: Charles Scribner's Sons, 1901]),
    pp. 180–82, http://www.hymntime.com.

Tracing God's Hand

1. Kester assumes there is a fragility for a family in much the same way as a human life is fragile. Since families can easily be broken, damaged, or destroyed just as human life can be, did this story recall to your mind instances of fragility you've seen? Would your response be different now?

2. In Lesson 4 of chapter 15 Kester states, "We can have unity without uniformity." Can you think of an example of this concept in your own life experiences?

3. Explain how love, death, and hope are
    interconnected in chapter 14 (the Christmas
    chapter) or in the work as a whole. What will
    you remember about Kester realizing this
    connection in her experience?

4. Regarding her decision on the importance of
    Scripture (Pivotal Decision Point 1 of chapter
    15), Kester quotes her husband: "I accept
    the Scripture as a mathematician accepts the
    axioms for the system he is going to work
    in." What other analogies can you think
    of to describe how Scripture functions for
    Christians?

5. What is the distinction between choosing
    to let God be in control (chapter 15, Pivotal
    Decision Point 3) and removing idols (chapter
    15, Pivotal Decision Point 4)? Was this

distinction evident in the Flashback chapter?
What idols do you recognize in your own life?
When have you chosen to let something go
and felt God's hand taking control?

6. Do you think Kester and her husband became
   more bold or confident after their wreck? What
   justification would you give for your answer?
   How will this help you as you face your own
   fears or as you help others face their fears?

7. Kester tells us that she overcame her own
   fearfulness, especially her fear for the safety and
   protection of her family and her fear of death.
   How would you explain this change?

8. We tend to want an immediate solution
    whenever we have a problem, but God does
    not necessarily work on our time frame. Did
    the book *Tracing God's Hand* give illustrations
    of a problem and its solution coming *with* each
    other from God's perspective—although not
    necessarily from our human perspective at the
    time of the problem? Explain how this will
    help you when facing problems in the future.

9. Do you think reading *Tracing God's Hand*
    will help you as you deal with difficult things
    happening in your own life in the future?
    Explain why or why not.

10. In what ways is a butterfly in metamorphosis a good illustration of experiencing grief?

11. In the Epilogue Kester states that her obedience to God in a particular situation before the wreck "became an entry point for His presence and power not only then, but later." How would you explain obedience to God being a catalysis in doing this? Can you identify such an "entry point" in your own life? Does the obedience illustrated in Jesus' parable of the two houses in Matthew 7:24–27 give you insight on this question?

12. In the Epilogue Kester describes how her husband was gradually shaped into a jewel over his lifetime. How do the difficulties a person goes through during their lifetime change them? How are you responding to your own difficulties in life?

13. What is the most important thing you personally take from reading this true story? How would you summarize it in one sentence or phrase?

14. How many parallels do you find between this true story you've read and Romans 5:1–5 below? What do you find?

> *Therefore, since we have been justified by faith, we have peace with God through our Lord Jesus Christ. Through him we have also obtained access by faith into this grace in which we stand, and we rejoice in hope of the glory of God. Not only that, but we rejoice in our sufferings, knowing that suffering produces endurance, and endurance produces character, and character produces hope, and hope does not put us to shame, because God's love has been poured into our hearts through the Holy Spirit who has been given to us.*
>
> (ROMANS 5:1–5)

ACKNOWLEDGMENTS

An author needs a supportive, nurturing community of friends and helpers to see a book idea flourish and develop into a reality, at least that's true for this one. Growing an idea into a book is hard work, and *Tracing God's Hand* wouldn't have happened without many of the friends I've made before and after moving to Westminster Canterbury in Lynchburg, Virginia.

First of all, I'm grateful that my husband nudged me to move and become a resident of the local Westminster Canterbury retirement community so, as he put it, "I would have time to write." Once settled into our new location, I joined the WC/ Virginia Episcopal School intergenerational Creative Writing group, where I received encouragement for my short family stories, a few of which I have incorporated into chapters of this book.

When the 2020 Covid lockdown arrived, Monty and I frequently looked through old pictures and traced how blessed we had been in our fifty-plus years of marriage. It was the perfect time to be writing *Tracing God's Hand* because that was exactly what we were doing. Two of my neighbors read some early chapters and began encouraging me to keep writing. After I completed my first draft, Jean and Charles Driscoll, Kriss and Harvey Hartman, Leona Choy, Lowell Sykes, and William Deal were kind enough to read and critique it. They enthusiastically encouraged me to enlarge my vision for the book. About this time I became a member of a writing group of eight called "Word Play." We met regularly, and they gave me valuable feedback as I began my final revisions.

Without the support of my peers, this book would not exist because Monty's unexpected death occurred as I completed the first draft. That could have derailed the whole book idea except for my many supportive and encouraging friends. Several personal friends and my Sunday School class began praying for my progress as I reworked the manuscript and struggled to write the epilogue in the midst of my grief.

People left flowers and notes at my door, and they gave words of encouragement in the elevator, in the hall, by phone, and by text. Although I have specifically named a few helpers, there is no way I could list everyone without the danger of missing someone, so I'll stop here. I am grateful to each in the community of individuals who have read parts of the story, prayed for me, or encouraged me along the journey. I deeply appreciate their help.

As for my professional helpers, I'm further indebted to Peter Lundell for his patient copyediting and all my team at Illumify. Special thanks for the vision of my editor, Geoffrey Stone, and the ever-patient Jen Clark and Lisa Hawker who guided me through the process. I'm also grateful for Michael Klassen, who initially showed such faith in *Tracing God's Hand* and introduced me to Illumify Media Global. Through their efforts this book came to life.

Most of all, I want to thank God. He is the center of my life and this story. Without Him, this book would not have happened.

ABOUT THE AUTHOR

PHYLLIS SMITH KESTER grew up mainly in Oklahoma before getting her BS and master's degrees at Oklahoma State University, where she met and married the love of her life. She had two sons who then gave her three grandsons. Phyllis had taught in Oklahoma, Texas, and Arkansas, and ended her teaching career teaching mathematics for twelve years at Liberty University in Virginia before retiring in 2000. Over the years she taught Sunday school, ladies' Bible studies, and hosted dinners in her home for young professionals seeking some challenging discussions over dinner. She and her husband often took in a young professional or college student to live with them as he/she transitioned a problematic time or recovered from an accident or surgery.

She and her husband team taught numerous conferences, weekend retreats, teacher in-service, and marriage seminars. While living in Texas, Phyllis opened and operated a Total Health Care business, and she and her husband developed and operated a Christian free–loan library in the Houston area of over 1000 books and 3000 audio tapes.

Phyllis loved planning adventure trips for the family, and during her empty–nest years she and her husband made memorable trips to many countries, which included China and a trip Brazil to celebrate a friend translating the Bible into a new language. They climbed mountains at Machu Picchu, Peru, after floating the Amazon. But one of her biggest thrills was the summer in Alaska when she and her husband visited the wild bears in their natural habitat for several days.

During the early years of marriage Phyllis wrote articles for a couple of newsletters and a local paper, as well as workshops she and her husband gave. In 1980 New Leaf Press saw a booklet she had written for her church and asked Phyllis to extend it into a book for them. New Leaf published *What's All This Monkey Business* in 1981, which sold out. When returning home from speaking at Concerned Women for America's 1985 convention in Washington, D.C. shortly before she was to publish a second book for New Leaf, Phyllis discovered her eldest teenage son needed closer supervision. Since family takes a higher priority, she laid aside writing to spend more attention and energy on teenage sons rather than writing and being preoccupied. She never regretted that decision.

Thank you for reading Tracing God's Hand.

Since book reviews help people locate books on the Internet, I would appreciate it if you would leave a short book review on Amazon and Goodreads. Please visit my website www.PhyllisKester.com to read some of my short stories and to find out about forthcoming books.

CPSIA information can be obtained
at www.ICGtesting.com
Printed in the USA
BVHW032317130223
658422BV00004B/86